accessible by design

A Comprehensive Guide to UX Accessibility for Designers

william webb

contents

introduction

importance of accessibility in ux design

Accessibility is a fundamental aspect of designing user experiences that are not only enjoyable but also inclusive. With the world becoming increasingly digital, it is essential to ensure that everyone can access and navigate digital spaces without barriers. This is where accessible UX design comes in. It helps create user experiences that cater to a wide range of users, including those with disabilities, ensuring no one is left behind.

One might ask, why should UX designers prioritize accessibility? The answer is simple: it's about empathy and inclusion. UX designers should strive to understand and address the needs of all users, regardless of their abilities or limitations. By considering accessibility from the very beginning, designers can create digital products that are genuinely inclusive and usable by everyone.

In addition to creating inclusive experiences, accessibility in UX design also provides several benefits. Here are some compelling reasons to prioritize accessibility:

1. Enhancing usability for everyone: Accessibility features designed for users with disabilities often benefit all users. For example, larger buttons and clear labels improve usability for everyone, including those with temporary or situational impairments, such as a broken arm or poor lighting conditions. By designing with accessibility in mind, UX designers can create user experiences that are more intuitive and enjoyable for everyone.
2. Expanding the user base: By making digital products accessible, businesses can tap into a larger market share. It is estimated that around 15% of the world's population experiences some form of disability. By ignoring accessibility, businesses are potentially excluding a significant portion of potential users. Accessible design helps expand the user base, leading to more potential customers and increased revenue.
3. Legal and ethical considerations: Many countries have enacted laws and regulations to ensure digital accessibility. For example, in the United States, the Americans with Disabilities Act (ADA) and Section 508 of the Rehabilitation Act require that digital content be accessible to individuals with disabilities. By adhering to accessibility guidelines, designers can help organizations avoid legal disputes and the negative publicity that comes with them.
4. Demonstrating social responsibility: Designing accessible products and services shows that a company cares about its users and is committed to social responsibility. This can enhance a company's reputation and make it more appealing to customers who value ethical and inclusive practices.

Now that we have established the importance of accessibility in UX design, let's look at some practical steps designers can take to create more accessible experiences:

- Familiarize yourself with accessibility guidelines: The Web Content Accessibility Guidelines (WCAG) are an excellent starting point for understanding the requirements of accessible design. By studying these guidelines and applying them to your designs, you can create digital products that are more accessible to users with disabilities.
- Include accessibility in the design process from the beginning: By considering accessibility early in the design process, you can make more informed decisions that lead to inclusive and usable products. By incorporating accessibility from the start, you also avoid the need for time-consuming and costly adjustments later on.
- Learn from users with disabilities: One of the best ways to understand the needs of users with disabilities is by involving them in the design process. By conducting usability tests and gathering feedback from users with different abilities, designers can gain valuable insights that inform their design decisions.
- Use accessible design patterns: Many common design patterns can be made more accessible with small adjustments. For example, ensuring that form fields have clear labels and are properly associated with their corresponding inputs can greatly improve the experience for users with assistive technologies like screen readers.
- Collaborate with other team members: Designing accessible products requires collaboration between designers, developers, content creators , and other

stakeholders. By working together, teams can ensure that accessibility considerations are addressed throughout the entire product lifecycle, from design and development to testing and maintenance. Encourage open communication and share knowledge about accessibility best practices among team members.

- Test for accessibility: In addition to involving users with disabilities in usability testing, make use of automated accessibility testing tools and manual testing techniques to ensure your designs meet accessibility standards. These tests can help identify potential issues and areas for improvement, allowing you to refine your design and ensure it is accessible to as many users as possible.
- Stay up to date on accessibility trends and advancements: The world of accessibility is constantly evolving, with new technologies, guidelines, and best practices emerging regularly. To stay current, make it a habit to follow industry experts, attend conferences or webinars, and read articles or blogs focused on accessibility. This will help you stay informed and apply the latest knowledge to your designs.

By prioritizing accessibility, you not only improve the lives of users with disabilities but also enhance the overall user experience for everyone. Accessible design is not just a moral or legal obligation; it is also a smart business strategy that leads to better products and happier users.

As you continue your journey in the world of accessible UX design, remember to keep empathy, inclusion, and usability at the heart of your work. By doing so, you will be well on your way to creating digital experiences that are truly accessible by design.

overview of the book and its objectives

By the end of this book, you should have a solid understanding of accessibility in UX design and the tools and techniques needed to create inclusive digital products.

Our primary objective is to empower you, the UX designer, with the knowledge and skills to design with accessibility in mind. By doing so, we aim to help you create digital products that cater to a diverse range of users, including those with disabilities. But before we dive into the specifics, let's take a moment to explore the structure of the book and the key topics we will cover.

This book is divided into three main parts, each focusing on a specific aspect of accessible UX design:

Part One: Understanding Accessibility

In the first part of the book, we will lay the foundation for understanding accessibility and its importance in UX design. We'll explore the concept of accessibility, discuss the different types of disabilities that can impact UX design, and delve into the business case for incorporating accessibility into your design process. By the end of this section, you should have a solid grasp of the fundamentals of accessibility and its relevance in the digital world.

Part Two: Designing for Accessibility

The second part of the book dives into the practical aspects of designing for accessibility. We'll cover key principles and best practices that can help you create user interfaces that are both visually appealing and accessible to a wide range of users. This section will address topics such as accessible typography, color and contrast, navigation, interaction, multimedia content, and responsive design. Throughout this part, you'll be introduced to various tools and techniques that you can apply to your own designs, ensuring they are accessible to as many users as possible.

Part Three: Evaluating and Implementing Accessibility

In the final part of the book, we'll focus on evaluating and implementing accessibility in your design process. We'll discuss different testing methods, such as automated and manual testing, as well as the importance of inclusive user testing. Additionally, we'll explore how to integrate accessibility into your design process from the very beginning, fostering collaboration between designers, developers, and content creators. Finally, we'll touch on accessibility laws and compliance, helping you understand the legal and ethical implications of accessible design.

Now that you have a general understanding of the structure of the book, let's delve into the specific objectives we aim to achieve:

1. Build a strong foundation in accessibility: We want to ensure that you have a thorough understanding of what accessibility entails and why it is essential in UX design. By grasping the fundamentals, you'll be better equipped to make informed design decisions that cater to a diverse range of users.
2. Develop practical design skills: We aim to provide you with actionable tools and techniques that you can apply directly to your designs. By learning and practicing these skills, you'll be able to create digital products that are both visually appealing and accessible to users with disabilities.
3. Foster a user-centered design approach: Throughout the book, we'll emphasize the importance of putting users at the center of your design process. By involving users with disabilities in usability testing and incorporating their feedback into your designs, you'll be better able to create digital products that are truly inclusive and meet the needs of all users.

4. Encourage collaboration and communication: Accessible design is a team effort, and we want to help you foster collaboration between designers, developers, and other stakeholders. By working together and sharing knowledge about accessibility best practices, you can create more accessible and inclusive digital products.
5. Understand legal and ethical implications: We aim to provide you with an understanding of the legal and ethical implications of accessibility in UX design. By being aware of the relevant laws and regulations, you can ensure that your designs meet legal requirements and avoid potential disputes or negative publicity.
6. Inspire a commitment to accessibility: Lastly, we hope to inspire you to become an advocate for accessibility within your organization and the broader UX community. By sharing your knowledge and promoting the importance of inclusive design, you can contribute to a more accessible and inclusive digital world.

As we progress through the sections of this book, we encourage you to keep these objectives in mind and actively apply the concepts and techniques you learn to your own design projects. By doing so, you'll not only gain a deeper understanding of the material but also see the tangible impact that accessible design can have on your digital products and the users who interact with them.

Remember that becoming proficient in accessible UX design is a journey, and this book is designed to be your guide along the way. As you grow and develop your skills, don't be afraid to ask questions, seek feedback, and continually refine your approach. It's through this process of exploration and learning that you'll truly become an expert in creating inclusive and accessible user experiences.

We hope that by the end of this book, you feel empowered to make a difference in the lives of all users, regardless of their abilities or limitations. Together, let's work towards a digital world where everyone can access and enjoy the benefits of technology without barriers.

With the book's structure and objectives now clear, we can embark on this exciting journey together. Get ready to immerse yourself in the world of accessible UX design, where empathy, inclusion, and usability are at the heart of every decision we make. We're confident that by the end of this book, you'll have the knowledge, skills, and passion to create digital experiences that are truly accessible by design.

how the book is structured

As mentioned in the previous section, the book is divided into three main parts, each focusing on a specific aspect of accessible UX design. This structure has been carefully crafted to facilitate a comprehensive understanding of the topic, starting with the foundational concepts and progressing to more advanced techniques and practical applications. Let's take a closer look at each part and the sections within them.

The first part of the book lays the groundwork for your journey into accessible UX design. It consists of three sections that will help you understand the basics of accessibility, its importance, and its relevance in the world of UX design.

1. The Basics of Accessibility: This section will introduce you to the concept of accessibility, providing an overview of the various standards and guidelines that inform accessible design. You'll learn about the role of UX designers in ensuring

accessibility and how it relates to the broader goals of user-centered design.

2. Disability Types and Their Impact on UX Design: In this section, we'll explore the different types of disabilities that can affect users' experiences with digital products. By understanding the unique needs and challenges faced by users with disabilities, you'll be better equipped to create designs that accommodate a diverse range of abilities.
3. The Business Case for Accessibility: This section highlights the benefits of incorporating accessibility into UX design from a business perspective. We'll discuss the legal, ethical, and financial reasons for making digital products accessible, as well as the positive impact it can have on brand reputation and customer satisfaction.

The second part of the book dives into the practical side of designing for accessibility. Across six sections, you'll learn about various design principles, best practices, and techniques that can be applied to create accessible and inclusive user experiences.

1. Accessible User Interface (UI) Design Principles: This section will introduce you to key principles that underpin accessible UI design, such as clarity, consistency, and flexibility. You'll learn how these principles can be applied to create user interfaces that are both visually appealing and accessible to users with disabilities.
2. Typography and Text Accessibility: In this section, we'll delve into the world of typography and text accessibility. You'll learn about best practices for font selection, sizing, and spacing, as well as the

importance of contrast and color in ensuring readability for all users.

3. Color and Contrast Accessibility: This section focuses on the role of color and contrast in accessible design. You'll discover how to choose accessible color palettes, ensure sufficient contrast, and utilize tools and techniques for evaluating color accessibility.
4. Accessible Navigation and Interaction: Here, we'll explore the importance of accessible navigation and interaction in UX design. You'll learn about keyboard accessibility, focus management, and accessible menus and navigation patterns, as well as best practices for designing accessible forms and controls.
5. Accessible Multimedia Content: In this section, we'll discuss the accessibility of multimedia content, such as images, videos, and audio files. You'll learn about providing text alternatives, captions, and transcripts, as well as how to create accessible animations and interactive elements.
6. Responsive and Adaptive Design for Accessibility: This section covers the importance of responsive and adaptive design in creating accessible user experiences. You'll learn how to design for different devices and screen sizes, as well as best practices for touch and gesture accessibility Part III: Evaluating and Implementing Accessibility
7. In the final part of the book, we'll focus on evaluating and implementing accessibility throughout your design process. Spanning four sections, this section will provide you with the tools and techniques needed to assess and refine your designs to ensure they meet accessibility standards and serve the needs of all users.

8. Testing and Evaluating Accessibility: This section will guide you through various methods for testing and evaluating the accessibility of your designs, including automated tools, manual testing techniques, and inclusive user testing. You'll learn how to identify and address potential accessibility issues to create a more inclusive digital product.
9. Integrating Accessibility into the Design Process: In this section, we'll discuss strategies for incorporating accessibility considerations into every stage of your design process, from planning and research to development and maintenance. You'll learn how to foster collaboration between designers, developers, and other stakeholders to create a more accessible and inclusive product.
10. Accessibility Laws and Compliance: This section will provide you with an overview of the legal landscape surrounding accessibility in UX design. You'll learn about relevant laws and regulations, as well as the importance of compliance and the potential consequences of non-compliance.
11. Advocating for Accessibility: The final section of the book will inspire you to become an advocate for accessibility within your organization and the broader UX community. You'll discover strategies for raising awareness, sharing knowledge, and promoting the importance of accessible design to create a more inclusive digital world.

With this detailed overview of the book's structure in hand, you are now better equipped to make the most of the content within each section. As you progress through the book, remember to revisit the objectives outlined in the previous section and reflect on how the material you are learning supports those goals.

We hope that this structure will enable you to develop a comprehensive understanding of accessible UX design, as well as the practical skills needed to create inclusive digital products. By following the roadmap laid out in this section, you'll be well on your way to becoming an expert in designing with accessibility in mind.

As we continue to explore the world of accessible UX design, keep in mind that your journey as a designer is an ongoing process of learning, experimenting, and refining your approach. Embrace the challenges and opportunities that come your way, and never stop seeking ways to make your designs more inclusive and accessible to all users. With this mindset and the knowledge gained from this book, you'll be well-equipped to create digital experiences that truly cater to the diverse needs and abilities of all users.

part one
understanding accessibility

1 / the basics of accessibility

definition and concept

IN THIS SECTION, we will delve into the definition and concept of accessibility, providing you with a solid foundation upon which to build your understanding of this critical aspect of UX design. By grasping these fundamental concepts, you will be better prepared to create digital products that are truly inclusive and cater to the diverse needs of all users.

At its core, accessibility is about ensuring that people with disabilities can perceive, understand, navigate, and interact with digital products, as well as contribute to them when applicable. This means that, as a UX designer, you need to consider the unique needs and challenges faced by users with disabilities when creating digital products, from websites and mobile apps to software applications and beyond.

To better understand the concept of accessibility, it's essential to be familiar with the four primary categories of disabilities that can impact a user's experience with digital products:

1. Visual Disabilities: Users with visual disabilities, such as blindness, low vision, or color blindness, may face challenges when interacting with digital

products that rely heavily on visual content. Designing for these users involves ensuring that all visual information is accessible through alternative means, such as text descriptions, appropriate color contrast, or compatibility with screen readers.

2. Auditory Disabilities: Users with auditory disabilities, including deafness or hearing impairment, may have difficulty perceiving audio content or distinguishing certain sounds. Designing for these users involves providing text alternatives for audio content, such as captions or transcripts, and considering the use of visual cues to supplement audio information.
3. Motor Disabilities: Users with motor disabilities, such as those with limited mobility, muscle weakness, or conditions that affect fine motor control, may struggle to interact with digital products that require precise movements or complex gestures. Designing for these users involves ensuring that all interactive elements are easy to use with a variety of input methods, such as keyboards, touchscreens, or assistive devices like switches or joysticks.
4. Cognitive Disabilities: Users with cognitive disabilities, which can include conditions such as learning disabilities, attention disorders, or memory impairments, may find it challenging to process, understand, or remember information presented in digital products. Designing for these users involves organizing content in a clear and logical manner, minimizing distractions, and providing support for various learning styles.

Now that we have a better understanding of the different types of disabilities that can affect a user's experience with digital products, let's explore some of the key principles that underpin accessible design. These principles serve as a foundation for creating user experiences that cater to the diverse needs and abilities of all users:

1. Perceivability: Inaccessible content is invisible to users with disabilities. To ensure that your digital product is perceivable, make certain that all information is available in a form that can be accessed by users with various disabilities. This might involve providing text alternatives for non-text content, ensuring sufficient color contrast, or using clear and concise language to convey information.
2. Operability: Users must be able to interact with your digital product, regardless of their abilities. To ensure operability, create user interfaces that are compatible with various input methods and devices, such as keyboards, touchscreens, or assistive technologies. Additionally, consider providing multiple ways for users to navigate and access content, such as through well-structured menus, search functionality, or clear and consistent navigation patterns.
3. Understandability: Users should be able to easily comprehend the content and interface of your digital product. To achieve understandability, use clear and concise language, organize content in a logical and consistent manner, and provide support for various learning styles. Additionally, ensure that interactive elements are predictable and easy to use, with clear labels and instructions.
4. Robustness: Your digital product should be compatible with a wide range of technologies, devices, and user preferences. To ensure robustness,

design your product to be adaptable and flexible, with support for various browsers, operating systems, and assistive technologies. Additionally, adhere to established standards and guidelines, such as the Web Content Accessibility Guidelines (WCAG), to promote compatibility and future-proof your designs.

These principles form the foundation of accessible design and should be kept in mind throughout every stage of the design process. By adhering to these principles, you can create digital products that are not only accessible to users with disabilities but also more usable and enjoyable for all users.

It's also important to recognize that accessibility is an ongoing process that involves continuous learning, testing, and refinement. As a UX designer, you should be prepared to iterate on your designs and seek feedback from users with diverse abilities to ensure that your digital products are truly inclusive.

As we move forward in our exploration of accessible UX design, keep these fundamental concepts and principles in mind. By understanding the diverse needs and challenges faced by users with disabilities and embracing the principles of accessible design, you will be better equipped to create digital products that are truly inclusive and accessible to all users.

In the upcoming sections, we'll delve deeper into the practical aspects of designing for accessibility, providing you with actionable strategies, techniques, and best practices to apply to your own design projects. By incorporating these insights into your design process, you will not only be able to create more accessible and inclusive digital products but also become a more empathetic and effective designer.

Let's continue our journey towards mastering accessible

UX design, with the knowledge that our efforts will make a tangible difference in the lives of countless users around the world. By embracing the principles of accessibility and striving to create digital experiences that cater to the diverse needs and abilities of all users, we can contribute to a more inclusive digital landscape where everyone has the opportunity to access and enjoy the benefits of technology.

standards and guidelines (wcag, ada, section 508)

In this section, we'll explore some of the most important standards and guidelines that govern accessibility in digital products, including the Web Content Accessibility Guidelines (WCAG), the Americans with Disabilities Act (ADA), and Section 508 of the Rehabilitation Act. By familiarizing yourself with these standards and guidelines, you'll be better equipped to create digital products that comply with legal requirements and meet the diverse needs of all users.

Web Content Accessibility Guidelines (WCAG)

The WCAG, developed by the World Wide Web Consortium (W3C), is a set of guidelines that provide a comprehensive framework for creating accessible web content. These guidelines have become the gold standard for web accessibility and are widely adopted by organizations around the world. The WCAG is organized around four guiding principles—perceivable, operable, understandable, and robust—which we discussed in the previous section.

The WCAG is periodically updated to reflect advancements in technology and best practices in accessible design. The most recent version, WCAG 2.2, is organized into three levels of conformance: A (lowest), AA (medium), and AAA (highest). While achieving AAA conformance is ideal, most organizations aim for at least AA conformance, as it is a more realistic and achievable target that still provides a high degree of accessibility.

Some of the key recommendations from the WCAG include:

1. Providing text alternatives for non-text content, such as images, videos, and audio files.
2. Ensuring that content is presented in a logical order and can be accessed using only a keyboard.
3. Providing clear and consistent navigation elements and labels.
4. Using appropriate color contrast and font sizes to ensure readability.
5. Providing captions, transcripts, and audio descriptions for multimedia content.

Americans with Disabilities Act (ADA)

The ADA is a federal law in the United States that prohibits discrimination against individuals with disabilities in all areas of public life, including employment, transportation, public accommodations, and telecommunications. Although the ADA was enacted in 1990, well before the rise of the internet, it has been increasingly interpreted to apply to digital products, such as websites and mobile apps.

Title III of the ADA, which focuses on public accommodations, has been the primary driver of accessibility-related lawsuits and settlements in the United States. Under Title III, businesses and organizations that serve the public are required to provide equal access to their goods and services, including those offered through digital channels. In the absence of specific web accessibility regulations under the ADA, courts and regulators often look to the WCAG as a benchmark for determining compliance.

Section 508 of the Rehabilitation Act

Section 508 is another key piece of accessibility legislation in the United States that specifically targets federal agencies and the technology they procure, develop, or use. Under Section 508, federal agencies are required to ensure that their electronic and information technology (EIT) is accessible to individuals with disabilities, including both employees and members of the public.

In 2018, Section 508 was updated to adopt the Web Content Accessibility Guidelines (WCAG) 2.0 Level AA as its standard for web accessibility, effectively aligning it with the global standard. This means that, in addition to following the WCAG, federal agencies must also comply with additional requirements that are specific to Section 508, such as providing accessible documentation and support services.

As a UX designer, it's crucial to familiarize yourself with these standards and guidelines and integrate them into your design process. By doing so, you'll not only create digital products that are more inclusive and accessible to all users but also minimize the risk of legal issues related to non-compliance.

In the sections ahead, we'll dive deeper into practical strategies and techniques for designing accessible digital products that adhere to these standards and guidelines. By putting these principles into practice, you'll be well on your way to becoming an expert in accessible UX design and creating digital experiences that truly cater to the diverse needs and abilities of all users.

Remember that understanding and implementing these standards and guidelines is not just about meeting legal requirements; it's about creating a more inclusive digital world. By making your digital products accessible to everyone, you're helping to break down barriers and create opportunities for individuals with disabilities to fully participate in and benefit from the digital landscape.

As we continue our journey through accessible UX design, let these standards and guidelines serve as a roadmap to guide your design decisions. They provide a wealth of valuable insights, best practices, and practical recommendations that you can apply to your own design projects. By adhering to these standards and guidelines, you'll not only create digital products that are more accessible and enjoyable for all users, but also contribute to a more inclusive digital ecosystem.

Let's press on with our exploration of accessible UX design, keeping in mind the vital role that these standards and guidelines play in shaping our design practices. By embracing these principles and striving to create digital experiences that cater to the diverse needs and abilities of all users, we can help ensure that everyone has the opportunity to access and enjoy the benefits of technology. Together, let's continue our journey towards a more accessible and inclusive digital world.

the role of ux designers in accessibility

In this section, we'll discuss the crucial role that UX designers play in making digital products accessible to everyone. By understanding your responsibilities and embracing accessibility as a core component of your design process, you'll be able to create digital experiences that are not only usable and enjoyable for all users but also help to build a more inclusive digital world.

As a UX designer, you have a unique opportunity to shape the way people interact with digital products. By focusing on the diverse needs and abilities of your users, you can create experiences that truly cater to everyone, including those with disabilities. This means going beyond simply meeting legal requirements or following accessibility guidelines. It's about recognizing that accessibility is an essential aspect of good design and prioritizing it throughout your design process.

Here are some key responsibilities and actions that UX designers can take to embrace accessibility in their work:

1. Educate yourself and stay informed: Understanding the diverse needs of users with disabilities and the various accessibility standards and guidelines is a crucial first step in creating accessible digital products. Invest time in learning about accessibility best practices, attend workshops or conferences, and stay up-to-date with the latest developments in the field.
2. Advocate for accessibility within your organization: As a UX designer, you can play a pivotal role in promoting accessibility within your team or organization. Encourage colleagues to prioritize accessibility, share resources and best practices, and work collaboratively to create a culture that values and supports inclusive design.
3. Involve users with disabilities in the design process: One of the most effective ways to create accessible digital products is by actively involving users with disabilities in your design process. Conduct usability tests with a diverse range of users, seek out their feedback, and incorporate their insights into your designs. This will help ensure that your digital products are truly inclusive and cater to the unique needs and abilities of all users.
4. Design for flexibility and adaptability: Accessibility is not a one-size-fits-all solution. Design your digital products to be flexible and adaptable to a wide range of user needs, preferences, and assistive technologies. This might involve offering multiple ways to navigate content, designing for various input methods, or ensuring compatibility with different browsers and operating systems.

5. Prioritize simplicity and clarity: A key aspect of accessible design is ensuring that your digital products are easy to understand and use, regardless of a user's abilities. Prioritize simplicity and clarity in your designs by using clear and concise language, organizing content in a logical and consistent manner, and providing clear labels and instructions for interactive elements.
6. Continuously evaluate and iterate on your designs: Accessibility is an ongoing process that requires continuous evaluation and refinement. Regularly assess the accessibility of your digital products, seek feedback from users with disabilities, and be prepared to iterate on your designs in response to their needs and challenges.

By embracing these responsibilities and actions, you can help to ensure that your digital products are accessible and inclusive to all users. As a UX designer, your role in promoting accessibility is essential, and by prioritizing it in your work, you'll not only create better digital experiences but also contribute to a more inclusive digital world.

As we continue our journey through the world of accessible UX design, let's remember the vital role that we, as UX designers, play in shaping the digital experiences of users with disabilities. By recognizing the diverse needs and abilities of all users and prioritizing accessibility in our design process, we can create digital products that are truly inclusive and enjoyable for everyone.

So, let's forge ahead in our quest to master accessible UX design, empowered by the knowledge that our efforts can make a meaningful difference in the lives of countless users around the globe. By embracing our role as advocates for accessibility and working tirelessly to create digital experiences that cater to the diverse needs and abilities of all users, we can contribute to a more inclusive and accessible digital landscape.

Remember that as UX designers, we have the power to shape the way people interact with technology and the digital world. By prioritizing accessibility and putting the needs of all users at the forefront of our design process, we can create digital products that are more usable, enjoyable, and inclusive. This, in turn, will help to break down barriers and create opportunities for individuals with disabilities to fully participate in and benefit from the digital world.

In the upcoming sections, we'll delve deeper into practical techniques and strategies for designing accessible digital products, providing you with the tools and knowledge you need to become an expert in accessible UX design. By applying these principles and techniques in your own design work, you'll be well on your way to creating digital products that are truly inclusive and accessible to all users.

So, let's continue our journey towards accessible UX design mastery, guided by the knowledge that our role as UX designers is crucial in creating a more inclusive digital world. Armed with the insights and best practices we've explored so far, we can work together to create digital experiences that are accessible and enjoyable for everyone

2 / disability types and their impact on ux design

vision impairments

WELCOME BACK, fellow designers! In this section, we'll focus on vision impairments and their impact on the user experience of digital products. By understanding the unique needs and challenges faced by users with vision impairments, you'll be better equipped to create digital experiences that are accessible and enjoyable for everyone.

Vision impairments encompass a wide range of conditions that affect a person's ability to see. These may include total blindness, low vision, color blindness, and other visual conditions. Each of these impairments presents unique challenges and requires specific considerations when designing digital products. Let's explore these impairments in more detail and discuss some strategies to address them in your designs.

1. Total blindness: Users who are totally blind rely on assistive technologies, such as screen readers, to access digital content. Screen readers convert on-screen text and elements into spoken words or Braille output, allowing users to navigate and interact with digital products without vision.

Design considerations for users who are totally blind:

- Use semantic HTML markup to ensure proper structure and hierarchy of content.
- Provide text alternatives for non-text content, such as images and multimedia.
- Ensure keyboard accessibility for all interactive elements.
- Use ARIA (Accessible Rich Internet Applications) attributes to provide additional context and information for screen reader users.
- Create consistent and predictable navigation elements.

1. Low vision: Users with low vision have some functional vision, but they may struggle to see small text, discern low-contrast elements, or navigate complex layouts. Low vision users may use assistive technologies such as screen magnifiers or adjust their device settings to improve visibility.

Design considerations for users with low vision:

- Use sufficient color contrast between text and background to improve readability.
- Provide resizable text that maintains its readability when enlarged.
- Design for various viewport sizes to accommodate users who zoom in or use screen magnifiers.
- Keep layouts simple and uncluttered, with a clear visual hierarchy.
- Offer multiple ways to access content, such as a table of contents or search functionality.

1. Color blindness: Color blindness affects the way users perceive colors, making it difficult for them to distinguish between certain colors, such as red and green or blue and yellow. This can impact their ability to understand visual cues and navigate digital products.

Design considerations for users with color blindness:

- Avoid using color as the sole means of conveying information. Instead, use additional visual cues, such as patterns, icons, or text labels.
- Test your designs with color blindness simulation tools to ensure that they remain clear and usable for users with color vision deficiencies.
- Choose color palettes that are easily distinguishable for users with different types of color blindness.

With these vision impairments in mind, let's explore some practical strategies to help you design more accessible digital products:

1. Perform accessibility audits: Regularly evaluate your designs for accessibility issues using automated tools, manual testing, and user feedback. This will help you identify and address potential barriers to accessibility for users with vision impairments.
2. Test with assistive technologies: Gain firsthand experience with assistive technologies, such as screen readers and screen magnifiers, to better understand the needs of users with vision impairments. Test your designs using these tools to ensure that they are compatible and usable.

3. Collaborate with users: Actively involve users with vision impairments in your design process through usability testing, interviews, and surveys. Their feedback and insights can help you uncover potential issues and create more inclusive designs.

As we continue to explore the world of accessible UX design, let's remember the importance of considering users with vision impairments in our design decisions. By understanding their unique needs and challenges, we can create digital products that are accessible and enjoyable for everyone.

With the knowledge and strategies we've discussed in this section, you're well on your way to designing digital experiences that are inclusive and accommodating for users with vision impairments. Keep these considerations in mind as you design, and remember that by prioritizing accessibility for users with vision impairments, you're not only creating better experiences for these users, but also contributing to a more inclusive digital world.

In the upcoming sections, we'll delve deeper into other types of disabilities and explore additional strategies and techniques for designing accessible digital products. As we continue our journey, let's remain committed to designing with accessibility at the forefront, ensuring that our digital creations cater to the diverse needs and abilities of all users.

So, let's forge ahead with our exploration of accessible UX design, guided by our newfound understanding of the unique needs and challenges faced by users with vision impairments. Together, let's strive to create digital experiences that are not only visually appealing but also truly accessible and enjoyable for everyone, regardless of their visual abilities.

hearing impairments

In this section, we will focus on hearing impairments and how they impact the user experience of digital products. By understanding the unique needs and challenges faced by users with hearing impairments, we can create digital experiences that are accessible and enjoyable for everyone.

Hearing impairments include a wide range of conditions that affect a person's ability to hear. These may range from mild hearing loss to profound deafness. Each of these impairments presents unique challenges and requires specific considerations when designing digital products. Let's explore these impairments in more detail and discuss some strategies to address them in your designs.

1. Mild to moderate hearing loss: Users with mild to moderate hearing loss may have difficulty hearing certain frequencies, understanding speech in noisy environments, or discerning soft sounds. They may rely on hearing aids, volume controls, or other assistive technologies to improve their listening experience.

Design considerations for users with mild to moderate hearing loss:

- Ensure that audio content can be easily controlled, such as adjusting volume or muting sound.
- Avoid autoplaying audio content, as this can be disorienting for users who rely on volume controls or hearing aids.
- Consider providing text transcripts for audio content to make it accessible for users with hearing impairments.

1. Severe to profound hearing loss or deafness: Users with severe to profound hearing loss or deafness may rely on visual or tactile cues to access digital content. They may use assistive technologies such as sign language interpretation, captions, or transcripts to understand spoken language.

Design considerations for users with severe to profound hearing loss or deafness:

- Provide captions or subtitles for video content, ensuring that they are accurate, synchronized, and appropriately styled for readability.
- Offer sign language interpretation for live events or video content when possible.
- Use clear and concise language in your content to aid comprehension for users who rely on text-based communication.

With these hearing impairments in mind, let's explore some practical strategies to help you design more accessible digital products:

1. Make multimedia content accessible: Ensure that all multimedia content, such as videos, podcasts, and live events, is accessible to users with hearing impairments. This can be achieved through the use of captions, transcripts, or sign language interpretation.
2. Use visual cues: Incorporate visual cues, such as icons or text labels, to support audio cues and convey important information. This can help users with hearing impairments better understand and navigate your digital products.

3. Avoid relying solely on sound: Ensure that your digital products do not rely exclusively on sound for functionality or the communication of important information. Provide alternative methods for users to access and interact with your content.
4. Test your designs with users: Involve users with hearing impairments in your design process through usability testing, interviews, and surveys. Their feedback and insights can help you uncover potential issues and create more inclusive designs.

As we continue to explore the world of accessible UX design, let's remember the importance of considering users with hearing impairments in our design decisions. By understanding their unique needs and challenges, we can create digital products that are accessible and enjoyable for everyone.

With the knowledge and strategies we've discussed in this section, you're well on your way to designing digital experiences that are inclusive and accommodating for users with hearing impairments. Keep these considerations in mind as you design, and remember that by prioritizing accessibility for users with hearing impairments, you're not only creating better experiences for these users, but also contributing to a more inclusive digital world.

In the upcoming sections, we'll delve deeper into other types of disabilities and explore additional strategies and techniques for designing accessible digital products. As we continue our journey, let's remain committed to designing with accessibility at the forefront, ensuring that our digital creations cater to the diverse needs and abilities of all users.

So, let's forge ahead with our exploration of accessible UX design, guided by our newfound understanding of the unique needs and challenges faced by users with hearing impairments. Together, let's strive to create digital experiences that are not only engaging and interactive but also truly accessible and enjoyable for everyone, regardless of their hearing abilities. By doing so, we will help shape a more inclusive digital landscape where all users can thrive and benefit from the wonders of technology.

As we progress in our journey to becoming accessibility champions, it's important to recognize the positive impact we can make on the lives of users with hearing impairments. By incorporating accessibility best practices and techniques into our design process, we can ensure that our digital creations are usable and enjoyable for all users, regardless of their individual abilities.

motor impairments

In this section, we will focus on motor impairments and their impact on the user experience of digital products. By understanding the unique needs and challenges faced by users with motor impairments, we can create digital experiences that are accessible and enjoyable for everyone.

Motor impairments encompass a wide range of conditions that affect a person's ability to move, control, or coordinate their body. These may include conditions such as muscular dystrophy, cerebral palsy, Parkinson's disease, or repetitive strain injuries. Each of these impairments presents unique challenges and requires specific considerations when designing digital products. Let's explore these impairments in more detail and discuss some strategies to address them in your designs.

1. Limited strength or dexterity: Users with limited strength or dexterity may struggle to perform precise movements or exert force, making it

difficult for them to use traditional input devices such as a mouse or keyboard.

Design considerations for users with limited strength or dexterity:

- Ensure that your digital products are fully keyboard accessible, as some users may rely on alternative input devices that emulate keyboard functionality.
- Design large, easily clickable targets for buttons and other interactive elements.
- Minimize the need for precise or complex gestures, such as dragging or pinching.
- Provide ample time for users to complete time-sensitive tasks.

1. Involuntary movements or tremors: Users with involuntary movements or tremors may have difficulty controlling their movements, making it challenging for them to interact with small or closely spaced elements on the screen.

Design considerations for users with involuntary movements or tremors:

- Create ample space between interactive elements to reduce the likelihood of accidental clicks or selections.
- Allow users to adjust the sensitivity of input devices to accommodate their level of motor control.
- Consider implementing features like "sticky keys" or "slow keys" to support users who have difficulty with simultaneous key presses or rapid input.

1. Limited mobility or range of motion: Users with limited mobility or range of motion may struggle to perform certain actions or reach specific areas of the screen.

Design considerations for users with limited mobility or range of motion:

- Design layouts that are easy to navigate, with important content and interactive elements placed within easy reach.
- Ensure that your digital products are compatible with alternative input devices, such as switches, sip-and-puff systems, or eye-tracking technologies.
- Avoid relying on hover or mouse-over interactions, as these may be difficult for users with limited mobility to perform.

With these motor impairments in mind, let's explore some practical strategies to help you design more accessible digital products:

1. Optimize for keyboard navigation: Ensure that your digital products can be easily navigated and interacted with using only a keyboard. This not only benefits users with motor impairments but also improves the overall usability of your products.
2. Provide customization options: Allow users to customize aspects of your digital products, such as input sensitivity, button size, or layout, to accommodate their individual needs and preferences.
3. Test with users: Involve users with motor impairments in your design process through

usability testing, interviews, and surveys. Their feedback and insights can help you uncover potential issues and create more inclusive designs.

As we continue to explore the world of accessible UX design, let's remember the importance of considering users with motor impairments in our design decisions. By understanding their unique needs and challenges, we can create digital products that are accessible and enjoyable for everyone.

With the knowledge and strategies we've discussed in this section, you're well on your way to designing digital experiences that are inclusive and accommodating for users with motor impairments. Keep these considerations in mind as you design, and remember that by prioritizing accessibility for users with motor impairments, you're not only creating better experiences for these users, but also contributing to a more inclusive digital world.

In the upcoming sections, we'll delve deeper into other types of disabilities and explore additional strategies and techniques for designing accessible digital products. As we continue our journey, let's remain committed to designing with accessibility at the forefront, ensuring that our digital creations cater to the diverse needs and abilities of all users.

So, let's forge ahead with our exploration of accessible UX design, guided by our newfound understanding of the unique needs and challenges faced by users with motor impairments. Together, let's strive to create digital experiences that are not only engaging and interactive but also truly accessible and enjoyable for everyone, regardless of their motor abilities. By doing so, we will help shape a more inclusive digital landscape where all users can thrive and benefit from the wonders of technology.

As we progress in our journey to becoming accessibility champions, it's important to recognize the positive impact we can make on the lives of users with motor impairments. By incorporating accessibility best practices and techniques into our design process, we can ensure that our digital creations are usable and enjoyable for all users, regardless of their individual abilities.

cognitive impairments

In this section, we'll turn our attention to cognitive impairments and their impact on the user experience of digital products. By understanding the unique needs and challenges faced by users with cognitive impairments, we can create digital experiences that are accessible and enjoyable for everyone.

Cognitive impairments encompass a wide range of conditions that affect a person's ability to process, understand, or remember information. These may include conditions such as autism, dyslexia, attention deficit hyperactivity disorder (ADHD), or traumatic brain injury. Each of these impairments presents unique challenges and requires specific considerations when designing digital products. Let's explore these impairments in more detail and discuss some strategies to address them in your designs.

1. Memory impairments: Users with memory impairments may struggle to recall information or remember how to perform certain tasks, making it difficult for them to navigate and use digital products effectively.

Design considerations for users with memory impairments:

- Use clear and consistent navigation patterns to help users orient themselves within your digital products.
- Provide reminders or prompts for important information, such as form input requirements or password guidelines.
- Offer easily accessible help documentation or tutorials to support users as they interact with your digital products.

1. Attention impairments: Users with attention impairments may have difficulty focusing on specific tasks or filtering out distractions, making it challenging for them to engage with digital products that require sustained attention.

Design considerations for users with attention impairments:

- Break complex tasks or content into smaller, manageable chunks to support users with limited attention spans.
- Minimize visual clutter and distractions, such as unnecessary animations or auto-playing media.
- Use clear, concise language and avoid long blocks of text to aid comprehension and maintain user engagement.

1. Processing impairments: Users with processing impairments may require more time to understand and interact with digital content, making it essential to create user experiences that are accommodating and supportive.

Design considerations for users with processing impairments:

- Ensure that your digital products are compatible with assistive technologies, such as screen readers or text-to-speech software.
- Provide ample time for users to complete time-sensitive tasks or interactions.
- Use clear headings and formatting to help users quickly identify and understand important information.

With these cognitive impairments in mind, let's explore some practical strategies to help you design more accessible digital products:

1. Simplify your designs: Create clean, simple layouts with clear navigation and minimal visual clutter to support users with cognitive impairments.
2. Use plain language: Write in a clear and concise manner, avoiding jargon and complex language whenever possible.
3. Provide alternative formats: Offer alternative formats for content, such as audio or video, to accommodate users with different cognitive abilities and preferences.
4. Test with users: Involve users with cognitive impairments in your design process through usability testing, interviews, and surveys. Their feedback and insights can help you uncover potential issues and create more inclusive designs.

As we continue to explore the world of accessible UX design, let's remember the importance of considering users with cognitive impairments in our design decisions. By understanding their unique needs and challenges, we can create digital products that are accessible and enjoyable for everyone.

With the knowledge and strategies we've discussed in this section, you're well on your way to designing digital experiences that are inclusive and accommodating for users with cognitive impairments. Keep these considerations in mind as you design, and remember that by prioritizing accessibility for users with cognitive impairments, you're not only creating better experiences for these users, but also contributing to a more inclusive digital world.

In the upcoming sections, we'll delve deeper into other types of disabilities and explore additional strategies and techniques for designing accessible digital products. As we continue our journey, let's remain committed to designing with accessibility at the forefront, ensuring that our digital creations cater to the diverse needs and abilities of all users.

So, let's forge ahead with our exploration of accessible UX design, guided by our newfound understanding of the unique needs and challenges faced by users with cognitive impairments. Together, let's strive to create digital experiences that are not only engaging and interactive but also truly accessible and enjoyable for everyone, regardless of their cognitive abilities. By doing so, we will help shape a more inclusive digital landscape where all users can thrive and benefit from the wonders of technology.

As we progress in our journey to becoming accessibility champions, it's important to recognize the positive impact we can make on the lives of users with cognitive impairments. By incorporating accessibility best practices and techniques into our design process, we can ensure that our digital creations are usable and enjoyable for all users, regardless of their individual abilities.

how to address different disability types in ux design

In this section, we'll explore how to address various disability types in UX design. As we've learned throughout this book, creating accessible digital products requires us to consider the unique needs and challenges of users with different abilities. By incorporating inclusive design principles into our work, we can create digital experiences that are accessible to everyone, regardless of their individual abilities.

In previous sections, we've covered specific disability types, such as vision impairments, hearing impairments, motor impairments, and cognitive impairments. Now, let's take a holistic approach and discuss some strategies that can help us create more accessible digital products for users with various disabilities.

1. Start with inclusive design principles: Inclusive design principles provide a strong foundation for creating accessible digital products that cater to the needs of all users. By following these principles, you can ensure that your digital products are flexible, adaptable, and accommodating for everyone. Some key inclusive design principles include:
2. Provide equitable use: Ensure that your digital products can be used by people with diverse abilities in a similar manner.
3. Allow flexibility in use: Offer multiple ways for users to interact with and access your digital products.
4. Keep it simple and intuitive: Design your digital products to be easy to understand and use, regardless of the user's experience or cognitive ability.

5. Use accessible design patterns: Familiarize yourself with common accessible design patterns and incorporate them into your work. These patterns can help you create digital products that are more accessible and usable for users with various disabilities. For example:
6. Use descriptive link text and button labels that clearly communicate the purpose or destination of the link or button.
7. Ensure that interactive elements have sufficient contrast and are easy to see and interact with.
8. Provide appropriate alternative text for images to convey their meaning or purpose to users with screen readers.
9. Test with a diverse group of users: Engage users with different disabilities in your design process through usability testing, interviews, and surveys. By involving users with diverse abilities in your design process, you can gain valuable insights, uncover potential issues, and create more inclusive digital products.
10. Ensure compatibility with assistive technologies: Many users with disabilities rely on assistive technologies, such as screen readers, text-to-speech software, or alternative input devices, to interact with digital products. Ensure that your designs are compatible with these technologies to provide an accessible experience for all users.
11. Create adaptable layouts and typography: Design your digital products to be flexible and responsive, allowing them to adapt to different devices, screen sizes, and user preferences. This includes using scalable typography, flexible layout systems, and providing options for users to adjust font sizes, colors, and other visual aspects.

Now, let's discuss some strategies for addressing the unique needs of users with different disability types in your UX design process:

1. Vision impairments: When designing for users with vision impairments, consider the following strategies:
2. Use sufficient color contrast to ensure text and interactive elements are easy to see.
3. Provide options for users to customize font size, color, and contrast.
4. Ensure that all content is accessible via screen readers, and use appropriate ARIA attributes to provide context and meaning.
5. Hearing impairments: To create accessible experiences for users with hearing impairments, consider these strategies:
6. Provide captions or transcripts for audio and video content.
7. Use clear, visual cues to convey important information or feedback, rather than relying solely on audio.
8. Ensure that any time-sensitive or interactive elements can be easily accessed and used without relying on audio cues.
9. Motor impairments: When designing for users with motor impairments, consider the following strategies:
10. Design large, easily tappable or clickable targets for interactive elements.

- Ensure that your digital products can be navigated using a keyboard or alternative input devices.
- Provide options for users to customize the level of interaction required, such as adjusting the amount

of time needed to complete time-sensitive tasks.

1. Cognitive impairments: To address the needs of users with cognitive impairments, consider these strategies:
2. Use clear, concise language and avoid jargon or complex terms.
3. Break complex tasks or content into smaller, manageable chunks.
4. Provide clear instructions and support, such as help documentation or tutorials, to guide users through the use of your digital products.

By keeping these strategies and considerations in mind, you can create digital products that are accessible and enjoyable for users with different disability types. Remember that the key to success in accessible UX design is understanding the unique needs of users with various abilities and incorporating inclusive design principles into your work.

As we continue our exploration of accessible UX design, let's remain committed to designing digital products that cater to the diverse needs and abilities of all users. By keeping the strategies and techniques we've discussed in this section in mind, you'll be well-equipped to create digital experiences that are inclusive and accommodating for users with different disability types.

In the upcoming sections, we'll delve deeper into additional strategies and techniques for designing accessible digital products, further expanding our understanding of this important topic. Together, let's continue to learn, grow, and make a positive impact on the lives of all users through our commitment to accessible UX design. By doing so, we'll not only improve the user experience for those with disabilities, but we'll also contribute to a more inclusive and accessible digital world for everyone.

3 / the business case for accessibility

legal requirements and risk management

WELCOME BACK, fellow designers! In this section, we'll dive into the legal requirements and risk management aspects of accessible UX design. While creating inclusive digital products is a moral and ethical responsibility, it's also important to understand the legal landscape surrounding accessibility to protect your organization and ensure compliance with relevant laws and regulations.

Let's first discuss some key legislation and guidelines that pertain to digital accessibility:

1. Web Content Accessibility Guidelines (WCAG): Developed by the World Wide Web Consortium (W3C), WCAG is a set of guidelines that provide a framework for creating accessible web content. WCAG is organized into three levels of conformance (A, AA, and AAA), with Level AA being the most widely recommended for compliance. These guidelines are internationally recognized and serve as a reference for many accessibility laws and policies around the world.

2. Americans with Disabilities Act (ADA): The ADA is a US civil rights law that prohibits discrimination against individuals with disabilities. While the ADA does not explicitly mention websites, court rulings and guidance from the Department of Justice have indicated that websites and digital products may be considered "places of public accommodation" and are thus subject to ADA compliance.
3. Section 508 of the Rehabilitation Act: This US federal law requires that electronic and information technology developed, procured, maintained, or used by the federal government be accessible to individuals with disabilities. Section 508 is aligned with WCAG 2.0 Level AA standards, which means that complying with WCAG 2.0 AA will generally satisfy Section 508 requirements.

Now that we've covered some of the key legislation and guidelines, let's discuss strategies for managing legal risks and ensuring compliance in your UX design process:

1. Develop an accessibility policy: Create a clear and comprehensive accessibility policy for your organization that outlines your commitment to digital accessibility and the steps you will take to ensure compliance with relevant laws and guidelines. This policy should be easily accessible and visible to both internal and external stakeholders.
2. Conduct accessibility audits: Regularly review your digital products to identify accessibility issues and areas of non-compliance. Use automated accessibility testing tools as well as manual testing and reviews by accessibility experts to ensure a

thorough evaluation. Document your findings and create a prioritized plan for addressing any issues.

3. Train your team: Provide ongoing training and education on accessibility best practices for your design and development teams. This will help ensure that all members of your team are familiar with the relevant guidelines and requirements, and are equipped to create accessible digital products.
4. Engage users with disabilities: Involving users with disabilities in your design and testing process can help identify potential issues and areas for improvement. These insights can be invaluable in ensuring that your digital products are not only compliant with relevant laws and guidelines but also truly accessible and usable for all users.
5. Document your efforts: Keep detailed records of your organization's accessibility efforts, including training sessions, audits, user feedback, and any remediation efforts. This documentation can be helpful in demonstrating your commitment to accessibility and compliance in case of any legal disputes or inquiries.
6. Stay informed: Laws and guidelines related to digital accessibility may evolve over time, so it's crucial to stay up-to-date on any changes and updates. Subscribe to newsletters, follow relevant organizations on social media, and participate in industry events to ensure you remain informed about the latest developments in accessibility legislation and best practices.

By adopting these strategies, you can effectively manage the legal risks associated with digital accessibility and ensure that your organization remains compliant with relevant laws and guidelines.

As we continue our journey through the world of accessible UX design, let's remember that our commitment to creating inclusive digital products is not only an ethical and moral responsibility but also a legal one.

enhancing brand reputation

In this section, we'll explore the connection between accessible UX design and brand reputation. As we've seen throughout this book, creating accessible digital products is not only a legal and moral imperative, but it can also have a significant impact on how your brand is perceived by users, stakeholders, and the wider public. By prioritizing accessibility, you can enhance your brand reputation, foster customer loyalty, and drive business success.

Let's discuss some of the ways in which accessible UX design can contribute to a positive brand image:

1. Demonstrating social responsibility: By designing digital products that are inclusive and accessible, you send a clear message that your brand is committed to social responsibility and values the experiences of all users, regardless of their abilities. This commitment can help to build trust and credibility among your target audience, who may be more inclined to support and engage with brands that prioritize accessibility and inclusivity.
2. Expanding your reach: Accessible design enables a broader range of users to access and interact with your digital products, including those with disabilities and older adults. By catering to the needs of these underserved populations, you can expand your customer base and tap into new markets, ultimately driving business growth and success.

3. Enhancing user experience for all: Inclusive design principles not only benefit users with disabilities but also lead to an improved user experience for everyone. By focusing on clarity, simplicity, and ease of use, accessible UX design can result in digital products that are more enjoyable and satisfying for all users, fostering greater customer satisfaction and loyalty.
4. Standing out from the competition: Embracing accessible UX design can help set your brand apart from competitors who may not prioritize accessibility. By promoting your commitment to accessibility in your marketing materials and showcasing the inclusive features of your digital products, you can differentiate your brand in a crowded marketplace and attract users who value accessibility.

Now that we understand the connection between accessible UX design and brand reputation, let's explore some strategies for leveraging accessibility to enhance your brand image:

1. Communicate your commitment: Make your dedication to accessibility known by including statements about your commitment to inclusive design on your website, in your marketing materials, and through your social media channels. By highlighting your accessibility efforts, you can demonstrate your brand's values and attract users who share those values.
2. Share success stories: Showcase the positive impact of your accessible digital products by sharing success stories, testimonials, or case studies from users with disabilities who have benefited from

your inclusive design efforts. These stories can help to humanize the accessibility work you've done and demonstrate its real-world impact.

3. Partner with accessibility advocates: Collaborate with organizations, influencers, or advocates within the disability community to amplify your accessibility message and further demonstrate your brand's commitment to inclusivity. This partnership can also provide valuable insights and guidance to inform your ongoing accessibility efforts.
4. Train your employees: Provide ongoing accessibility training for your team, ensuring that all staff members understand the importance of accessibility and have the skills and knowledge necessary to create inclusive digital products. This training can help to create a culture of accessibility within your organization and ensure that your commitment to accessibility is reflected across all aspects of your brand.
5. Continuously improve and innovate: Accessibility is an ongoing process, and it's essential to regularly evaluate your digital products and make improvements based on user feedback, technological advancements, and evolving best practices. By consistently working to enhance the accessibility of your digital products, you can demonstrate your brand's commitment to continuous improvement and innovation.

By implementing these strategies, you can effectively leverage accessible UX design to enhance your brand reputation and drive business success. Remember, prioritizing accessibility not only benefits users with disabilities but also has the potential to improve the user experience for everyone, resulting in a stronger, more positive brand image.

In summary, accessible UX design can play a crucial role in enhancing your brand's reputation. By demonstrating a commitment to social responsibility, expanding your reach, improving the user experience for all, and differentiating your brand from competitors, you can elevate your brand's image and foster customer loyalty.

As we continue to explore the world of accessible UX design, let's remember that our work has the potential to make a significant impact not only on the lives of individual users but also on the broader perception of our brands. By prioritizing accessibility and inclusivity, we can create digital products that not only meet legal requirements but also contribute to a positive brand image that resonates with users and stakeholders alike.

expanding market reach

In this section, we'll focus on the importance of accessible UX design in expanding your market reach. By designing digital products that cater to the needs of diverse users, including those with disabilities, you can tap into new markets and attract a wider audience. Let's explore how accessibility can contribute to market expansion and the practical steps you can take to broaden your user base.

When discussing market reach, it's crucial to understand the size of the population that could benefit from accessible UX design. The World Health Organization estimates that over a billion people live with some form of disability, which is approximately 15% of the world's population. By designing digital products that are accessible and inclusive, you can potentially reach this sizable demographic, which is often underserved by mainstream design practices.

In addition to users with disabilities, accessible UX design can also benefit other populations, including:

1. Aging population: As the global population ages, the number of older adults with age-related impairments is also increasing. Accessible design can help address the needs of this growing demographic by ensuring that digital products are usable by people with reduced vision, hearing, mobility, or cognitive abilities.
2. Users with situational impairments: Situational impairments can occur when users face temporary limitations due to their environment or circumstances, such as using a mobile device in bright sunlight, or having a broken arm. Accessible design can help accommodate these users by providing flexible and adaptable interfaces.
3. Users with varying levels of digital literacy: Accessible design can also benefit users who may not be as familiar with technology, including those who have limited experience or are new to digital products. By prioritizing clarity and simplicity, accessible UX design can help bridge the digital divide and make products more approachable for all users.

Now that we understand the potential benefits of accessible UX design for expanding market reach, let's discuss some strategies to make your digital products more inclusive and accessible:

1. Conduct user research: Start by conducting user research to identify the needs and preferences of your target audience, including users with disabilities. This research can help you understand the specific accessibility requirements of your users and inform your design decisions.

2. Adopt a universal design approach: Universal design is an approach that aims to create products that are usable by the widest possible audience, without the need for adaptation or specialized design. By incorporating universal design principles into your UX design process, you can create digital products that are more likely to be accessible to a broad range of users.
3. Follow accessibility guidelines: Adhere to established accessibility guidelines, such as WCAG, to ensure that your digital products meet the minimum accessibility requirements. These guidelines provide a framework for creating accessible web content and can help you identify potential barriers to access.
4. Test your designs with diverse users: Engage users with different abilities in the testing and evaluation of your digital products. This can help you identify any accessibility issues and ensure that your designs are truly inclusive and usable by a wide range of users.
5. Implement a continuous improvement process: Accessibility is an ongoing process that requires regular evaluation and refinement. Monitor user feedback and analytics to identify any areas of your digital products that may need improvement and make the necessary updates to ensure that your products remain accessible and inclusive.

By implementing these strategies, you can create digital products that cater to the needs of diverse users and expand your market reach. As a result, your brand can attract a wider audience, drive business growth, and foster customer loyalty.

In conclusion, accessible UX design plays a vital role in expanding market reach and ensuring that digital products are inclusive and usable by all users, regardless of their abilities. By focusing on the needs of diverse users, including those with disabilities, you can tap into new markets, foster customer loyalty, and drive business success. Remember that designing with accessibility in mind not only benefits users with disabilities but also contributes to a better user experience for everyone, ultimately leading to a more inclusive and accessible digital world.

As we move forward in our journey to create more accessible digital products, let's continue to prioritize the needs of diverse users and strive to make our designs as inclusive as possible. By doing so, we can effectively expand our market reach, create a positive impact on the lives of all users, and position our brands for long-term success.

improving overall user experience

In this section, we'll discuss the ways in which accessible UX design can lead to an improved user experience for all. Designing with accessibility in mind not only benefits users with disabilities, but it can also have a positive impact on the experience of a broader range of users. Let's dive into the various ways accessible design contributes to an enhanced user experience and explore the best practices to achieve this goal.

One of the key principles of accessible design is ensuring that digital products are easy to use and understand. This focus on simplicity and clarity can benefit all users, not just those with disabilities. By prioritizing ease of use, your designs can become more approachable and enjoyable for a wide range of users, leading to increased satisfaction and engagement.

Here are some ways in which accessible UX design can contribute to an improved overall user experience:

1. Better navigation and structure: Accessible design often involves creating clear, consistent, and well-organized navigation systems. This can help all users quickly find the information they need and navigate your digital products with ease.
2. Improved readability: Accessible design principles emphasize the importance of clear, legible text and adequate contrast between text and background colors. By following these guidelines, you can make it easier for all users to read and understand your content, regardless of their visual abilities.
3. Enhanced usability: Accessible UX design frequently involves designing for a wide range of input methods, such as keyboard navigation, touchscreens, and voice commands. By accommodating these different input methods, you can create digital products that are more usable by all users, regardless of their individual preferences or abilities.
4. Flexible and adaptable interfaces: Accessible design often requires creating interfaces that can adapt to different user needs, preferences, and devices. This flexibility can benefit all users by providing a more personalized and enjoyable experience.
5. Reduced cognitive load: By prioritizing simplicity and clarity, accessible design can help reduce the cognitive load on users, making it easier for them to understand and interact with your digital products.

Now, let's discuss some best practices for implementing accessible UX design to improve the overall user experience:

1. Use clear and concise language: Write content that is easy to understand and avoid using jargon or complex terminology. By keeping your language

simple and concise, you can ensure that your content is accessible to a wide range of users, including those with cognitive impairments or limited language proficiency.

2. Provide clear and consistent navigation: Design navigation systems that are easy to understand and use. Consistency in navigation structure, labeling, and visual presentation can help users quickly find the information they need and reduce the likelihood of confusion or frustration.
3. Use meaningful headings and labels: Organize your content using clear, descriptive headings and labels that accurately reflect the content they represent. This can help users quickly scan your content and find the information they need.
4. Ensure sufficient color contrast: Choose text and background colors that provide adequate contrast, making it easier for users with low vision or color vision deficiencies to read your content. You can use online tools like the WebAIM Color Contrast Checker to ensure your color choices meet accessibility guidelines.
5. Design for different input methods: Ensure your digital products are usable with a variety of input methods, including keyboard navigation, touchscreens, and voice commands. This can help accommodate users with different preferences or abilities and contribute to a more inclusive user experience.
6. Provide alternative text for images: Include descriptive alternative text for all images, which can be read by screen readers to convey the meaning of the image to users who are blind or visually impaired. This not only benefits users with disabilities but also provides additional context for

all users, particularly when images fail to load or are turned off.

By incorporating these best practices into your UX design process , you can create digital products that are more inclusive, enjoyable, and easy to use for a diverse range of users. Ultimately, accessible design is about putting the needs and preferences of users at the forefront of your design decisions, resulting in a better user experience for all.

Furthermore, designing for accessibility can lead to some unexpected benefits, such as improved performance, better search engine optimization (SEO), and increased adaptability to new technologies and devices. For example, by creating websites that load quickly and efficiently, you can enhance the experience for users with slow internet connections or limited data plans. Similarly, by following accessible design principles, your content is more likely to be well-structured and easily understood by search engines, leading to higher search rankings.

It's important to remember that accessibility should not be an afterthought or a separate consideration in the design process. Instead, integrating accessibility from the beginning of the project can lead to more cohesive and user-friendly designs. By considering the needs and preferences of a diverse range of users from the outset, you can create digital products that are truly inclusive and enjoyable for everyone.

In this section, we've discussed the various ways in which accessible UX design can lead to an improved overall user experience. By adopting accessible design principles and incorporating them into your design process, you can create digital products that are not only more inclusive but also more enjoyable and satisfying for all users.

As we progress through the book, we'll continue to explore practical techniques and best practices for accessible UX design. Our goal is to equip you with the knowledge and skills needed to create digital products that cater to the needs of a wide range of users, contributing to a more inclusive and accessible digital landscape.

Let's continue our journey together, embracing accessibility as a core component of our design practice and working towards a digital world that is welcoming and enjoyable for everyone.

part two
designing for accessibility

4 / accessible user interface (ui) design principles

clarity and simplicity

HELLO AGAIN, fellow designers! In this section, we will delve into the importance of clarity and simplicity in UX design, particularly when it comes to creating accessible digital products. These principles help ensure that our designs are easy to understand and navigate for users of all abilities. By focusing on clear and straightforward design elements, we can create an inclusive and enjoyable user experience for everyone.

First, let's discuss why clarity and simplicity are crucial for accessible UX design:

1. Reducing cognitive load: Cognitive load refers to the mental effort required to process information and complete tasks. By simplifying our designs and making them clear, we can reduce the cognitive load on users, making it easier for them to understand and interact with our digital products.
2. Benefiting users with cognitive impairments: Users with cognitive impairments, such as dyslexia or attention deficit disorder, may struggle with

complex interfaces and dense information. Clarity and simplicity can help make our designs more accessible to these users by reducing potential barriers to understanding and interaction.

3. Improving usability for all users: Simplifying our designs not only benefits users with disabilities but also enhances the user experience for everyone. Clear and easy-to-use interfaces are more enjoyable and efficient for all users, regardless of their abilities.

Now that we understand the importance of clarity and simplicity, let's explore some practical strategies for incorporating these principles into our designs:

1. Use clear and concise language: Ensure that the text in your designs is easy to read and understand. Avoid jargon, technical terms, and lengthy sentences. Instead, use simple, everyday language that is familiar to your target audience. Additionally, consider providing alternative text for images and other non-text elements to improve accessibility for users who rely on screen readers or have difficulty interpreting visual content.
2. Organize content logically: Arrange the information on your site or application in a logical, easy-to-follow manner. Use headings and subheadings to break up content and create a clear hierarchy. This not only makes it easier for users to find what they're looking for but also improves the experience for those using assistive technologies, such as screen readers.
3. Minimize visual clutter: Avoid overwhelming users with excessive visual elements, such as images, animations, or decorative elements. Instead, focus

on presenting essential information in a clean and straightforward layout. This will help reduce cognitive load and make it easier for users to locate and interact with the content they need.

4. Prioritize functionality over aesthetics: While it's important for our designs to be visually appealing, it's crucial to prioritize usability and accessibility. Ensure that your design choices don't compromise clarity or simplicity. For example, if a particular font or color scheme looks great but is difficult to read, it's not an appropriate choice for an accessible design.
5. Optimize navigation: Make it easy for users to navigate your site or application by providing clear and consistent navigation elements. Use descriptive labels for buttons and links, and ensure that the overall navigation structure is intuitive and easy to understand.
6. Provide clear feedback and error messages: Help users understand the consequences of their actions and guide them through the process of correcting any mistakes. Use clear, informative messages to indicate when an action is successful or when an error has occurred. This is particularly important for users with cognitive impairments, who may struggle to interpret ambiguous feedback.
7. Test and iterate: Regularly test your designs with users of varying abilities to identify areas that may be confusing or difficult to navigate. Use the feedback you receive to refine your design and make it clearer and more straightforward for all users.

By incorporating these strategies into your design process, you can create digital products that are both visually appealing and accessible to users of all abilities. Clarity and simplicity are essential aspects of accessible UX design nd can make a significant difference in the overall user experience.

Remember, as UX designers, our primary goal is to make our digital products easy to use and understand for everyone. Clarity and simplicity are not just for users with disabilities but for all users who interact with our designs. By following these principles, we can create a more inclusive, user-friendly, and accessible digital environment.

As we move forward in our journey to become better UX designers, let's keep the following takeaways in mind:

1. Clarity and simplicity are essential components of accessible UX design, benefiting users with cognitive impairments and improving usability for all users.
2. Use clear and concise language, organize content logically, and minimize visual clutter to reduce cognitive load and make your designs easier to understand and navigate.
3. Prioritize functionality over aesthetics, optimize navigation, and provide clear feedback and error messages to enhance the overall user experience.
4. Regularly test your designs with users of varying abilities and iterate based on their feedback to continuously improve the clarity and simplicity of your digital products.

By integrating these principles into your design practice, you can make a positive impact on the lives of countless users, regardless of their abilities or limitations. In the end, the goal is to create digital products that empower and engage users while promoting inclusivity and accessibility.

consistency and predictability

Hello, fellow designers! In this section, we will focus on two essential principles in UX design that contribute to accessible and inclusive digital experiences: consistency and predictability. By ensuring our designs are consistent and predictable, we can create an environment that is easier to understand and navigate for users of all abilities. Let's dive in and explore why consistency and predictability are crucial for accessibility and how we can effectively incorporate these principles into our designs.

The importance of consistency and predictability in accessible UX design:

1. Reducing cognitive load: Similar to clarity and simplicity, consistency and predictability help to reduce cognitive load for users by establishing familiar patterns and structures in our designs. When users can easily anticipate how a digital product will function, they can focus their mental energy on the task at hand rather than trying to decipher unfamiliar elements.
2. Supporting users with cognitive impairments: Users with cognitive impairments, such as memory issues or difficulty processing information, can benefit greatly from consistent and predictable designs. These users often rely on familiar patterns and structures to help them navigate digital products successfully.
3. Enhancing usability for all users: Consistency and predictability are beneficial for all users, not just those with disabilities. When a digital product is consistent and predictable, users can quickly learn how to use it, leading to a more efficient and enjoyable experience for everyone.

Now that we understand the importance of consistency and predictability let's discuss some strategies for incorporating these principles into our designs:

1. Maintain a consistent visual design: Ensure that your visual design elements, such as colors, fonts, and icons, are consistent across your digital product. This helps to create a cohesive experience and allows users to quickly recognize and understand the various components of your interface.
2. Use consistent language and terminology: Just as important as visual consistency is the consistency of language and terminology. Be sure to use the same terms and phrases throughout your digital product to avoid confusion and make it easier for users to understand and navigate.
3. Establish consistent navigation: Create a consistent navigation structure that remains the same throughout your digital product. This helps users build a mental model of your interface, making it easier for them to find the information they need and complete tasks more efficiently.
4. Develop predictable interaction patterns: Ensure that interactive elements, such as buttons and links, behave in predictable ways. For example, a button should always trigger the same action, and links should consistently navigate users to a new page or section. By creating predictable interaction patterns, users can more easily understand how to interact with your digital product.
5. Provide consistent feedback: Consistently provide feedback to users about the results of their actions, such as successful form submissions or error messages. This helps users understand what is

happening within your digital product and ensures they can take the appropriate steps to complete their tasks successfully.

6. Test and iterate: Regularly test your designs with users of varying abilities to ensure that they are consistent and predictable. Use the feedback you receive to refine your designs and make them more accessible for everyone.

By incorporating these strategies into your design process, you can create digital products that are consistent and predictable, leading to more accessible and enjoyable experiences for all users.

As we progress in our journey to become better UX designers, let's remember the following key takeaways:

1. Consistency and predictability are essential aspects of accessible UX design, helping to reduce cognitive load and support users with cognitive impairments.
2. To create consistent and predictable designs, maintain a consistent visual design, use consistent language and terminology, establish consistent navigation, develop predictable interaction patterns, and provide consistent feedback.
3. Test your designs regularly with users of varying abilities and use their feedback to refine your designs and ensure they are consistent and predictable.

Incorporating consistency and predictability into your design practice not only benefits users with disabilities but also enhances the overall user experience for everyone. When digital products are consistent and predictable, users can navigate them more efficiently, feel more confident in their interactions, and ultimately enjoy a more satisfying experience.

As we wrap up this section, let's continue building on our understanding and expertise in creating accessible digital experiences. With consistency and predictability as a strong foundation, we can work together to design digital products that are not only inclusive and accessible but also provide a delightful and engaging user experience for all.

In the upcoming sections, we will further explore additional principles and techniques that can help us design more accessible digital products. Our collective efforts as UX designers play a crucial role in shaping the digital world and ensuring that it is a welcoming, inclusive space for everyone, regardless of their abilities or limitations.

flexibility and adaptability

In this section, we'll explore the important principles of flexibility and adaptability in UX design. By creating digital products that are flexible and adaptable, we can cater to a diverse range of users with varying needs, preferences, and abilities. This not only helps us design more accessible experiences but also ensures that our digital products can grow and evolve along with our users. Let's dive in and discover why flexibility and adaptability are essential for accessible UX design and how we can incorporate these principles into our work.

The importance of flexibility and adaptability in accessible UX design:

1. Accommodating diverse users: Flexibility and adaptability enable us to design digital products that cater to a wide range of users, including those with disabilities. By considering the diverse needs and preferences of our users, we can create

experiences that are more inclusive and accessible for everyone.

2. Adjusting to user preferences: When our digital products are flexible and adaptable, users can easily customize their experience to suit their preferences. This allows them to interact with our products in a way that is comfortable and efficient for them, enhancing their overall experience.
3. Future-proofing our designs: As technology continues to evolve, so do the needs and expectations of our users. By designing flexible and adaptable digital products, we can ensure that they remain relevant and accessible as new technologies and user needs emerge.

Now that we understand the importance of flexibility and adaptability, let's discuss some strategies for incorporating these principles into our designs:

1. Offer multiple ways to complete tasks: Provide users with different options for completing tasks, such as using a mouse, keyboard, or touch screen. This allows users to choose the method that works best for them, taking into account their abilities and preferences.
2. Design for scalability: When designing digital products, consider how they might need to grow or evolve in the future. Ensure that your design can accommodate new features, content, or user needs without compromising accessibility.
3. Support customization: Allow users to customize their experience by offering options for adjusting font size, color contrast, or other elements that impact accessibility. This enables users to create an

experience that meets their unique needs and preferences.

4. Utilize responsive design: Responsive design ensures that your digital product adapts to different screen sizes and devices, making it more accessible to a diverse range of users. By incorporating responsive design principles, you can create a seamless experience across various platforms and devices.
5. Adopt progressive enhancement: Progressive enhancement is a design strategy that prioritizes core functionality and content while gradually adding more advanced features and enhancements. This approach ensures that your digital product remains accessible to users with different abilities and devices, even if they can't access all of the advanced features.
6. Test and iterate with diverse users: Regularly test your designs with users who have different abilities, preferences, and needs. Use their feedback to refine your designs, making them more flexible and adaptable for a wider audience.

By incorporating these strategies into your design process, you can create digital products that are both flexible and adaptable, leading to more accessible and enjoyable experiences for all users.

As we continue our journey to become better UX designers, let's keep the following key takeaways in mind:

1. Flexibility and adaptability are essential aspects of accessible UX design, helping to accommodate diverse users and adjust to their preferences.
2. To create flexible and adaptable designs, offer multiple ways to complete tasks, design for

scalability, support customization, utilize responsive design, adopt progressive enhancement, and test and iterate with diverse users.

3. Embracing flexibility and adaptability in our design practice not only benefits users with disabilities but also enhances the overall user experience for everyone.

As we progress through our exploration of accessible UX design, let's remember the importance of flexibility and adaptability in creating inclusive and accessible digital experiences. By prioritizing these principles, we can ensure that our designs cater to a diverse range of users, providing a positive experience for all.

In the coming sections, we'll delve deeper into additional strategies and techniques that can help us design digital products that are even more accessible and enjoyable for our users. As we continue to learn and grow as UX designers, it's essential to remember the importance of flexibility and adaptability in shaping the digital world.

Let's move forward together, armed with the knowledge and understanding of how vital flexibility and adaptability are in creating inclusive digital experiences. By incorporating these principles into our design practice, we can work towards a more accessible digital landscape where everyone, regardless of their abilities or limitations, can engage with and enjoy the products we create.

As we continue to refine our designs and broaden our understanding of accessible UX design, we must always strive to be adaptable and open to change. The digital world is constantly evolving, and as UX designers, we must be prepared to evolve with it. By staying curious and embracing the principles of flexibility and adaptability, we can ensure that our designs remain relevant, user-friendly, and, most importantly, accessible to all.

feedback and error management

In this section, we'll be discussing the critical topic of feedback and error management in UX design. As designers, our goal is to create seamless, user-friendly experiences. However, we must also accept that users will inevitably encounter errors or issues when using our products. When these situations arise, it's essential to provide users with clear feedback and help them recover from errors quickly and efficiently. Let's explore the importance of feedback and error management in accessible UX design and learn some strategies for implementing these concepts into our designs.

The importance of feedback and error management in accessible UX design:

1. Reducing frustration: Encountering errors or issues can be frustrating for users. By providing clear feedback and guidance on how to resolve these problems, we can minimize user frustration and create a more enjoyable experience.
2. Ensuring a smooth user experience: Effective feedback and error management can help users recover from errors quickly and easily, preventing them from becoming stuck or disoriented in the process.
3. Enhancing accessibility: For users with disabilities, understanding and resolving errors may be particularly challenging. By implementing effective feedback and error management strategies, we can create a more accessible experience for all users.

Now that we understand the importance of feedback and error management, let's discuss some techniques for incorporating these principles into our designs:

1. Provide clear and immediate feedback: When users interact with your digital product, it's essential to provide clear and immediate feedback on the results of their actions. This can be done through visual cues, such as highlighting a selected button, or auditory feedback, such as a sound effect when an action is completed.
2. Use informative error messages: When users encounter an error, provide them with clear, concise, and informative error messages. These messages should explain the nature of the error and, if possible, offer guidance on how to resolve the issue.
3. Design for error prevention: While it's essential to help users recover from errors, it's even better to prevent errors from occurring in the first place. Consider designing your digital product in a way that minimizes the likelihood of user errors, such as providing clear instructions or implementing input validation.
4. Offer multiple methods for error recovery: When errors do occur, provide users with multiple methods for resolving the issue. This might include offering a "back" button to return to the previous screen or suggesting alternative actions the user can take to achieve their goal.
5. Make error recovery accessible: Ensure that your error recovery methods are accessible to users with disabilities. For example, include descriptive text for screen readers when presenting visual error messages or provide alternative methods for resolving errors that don't rely solely on visual cues.
6. Test and refine: Regularly test your designs with users, paying particular attention to feedback and

error management. Use their feedback to identify areas for improvement and refine your designs accordingly.

By incorporating these strategies into your design process, you can create digital products that effectively manage feedback and errors, leading to more accessible and enjoyable experiences for all users.

As we continue our exploration of accessible UX design, let's keep the following key takeaways in mind:

1. Feedback and error management are essential aspects of accessible UX design, helping to reduce user frustration and ensure a smooth user experience.
2. To implement effective feedback and error management, provide clear and immediate feedback, use informative error messages, design for error prevention, offer multiple methods for error recovery, make error recovery accessible, and test and refine your designs.
3. By focusing on feedback and error management, we can create more accessible and user-friendly digital products, enhancing the overall experience for all users.

As we progress through our journey towards becoming better UX designers, let's remember the importance of feedback and error management in creating accessible digital experiences. By incorporating these principles into our design practice, we can ensure that our digital products are not only visually appealing and functional but also accessible and user-friendly for everyone.

In the upcoming sections, we will dive deeper into various aspects of accessible UX design, covering topics such as assistive technologies, user testing, and inclusive design processes. As we continue to learn and grow as UX designers, let's keep the importance of feedback and error management in mind, striving to create digital products that are accessible and enjoyable for all users.

Let's keep moving forward, building on our understanding of feedback and error management, and applying these concepts in our designs. Together, we can work towards a more inclusive digital landscape, where everyone can navigate and engage with the digital products we create, regardless of their abilities or limitations.

As we continue to develop our skills and knowledge as UX designers, let's always be mindful of the role that feedback and error management play in accessible design. The digital world is ever-changing, and it's our responsibility to stay informed, adaptable, and committed to creating a more accessible environment for all users.

5 / typography and text accessibility

font selection

FONT SIZE and spacing are two crucial aspects of UX design that significantly impact the readability and accessibility of digital content. In this section, we'll delve into the importance of font size and spacing, discuss guidelines and best practices, and share tips to help you make informed decisions for your designs.

Font size plays a pivotal role in making your digital content easy to read and understand. When selecting the appropriate font size, it's essential to consider the needs of your users, especially those with visual impairments. A font that's too small can make the content difficult to read and cause strain on users' eyes, while overly large text can be visually overwhelming and impact the overall layout of your design.

To ensure that your content is accessible and legible, follow these general font size guidelines:

1. Body text: Aim for a minimum of 16 pixels for body text on desktop devices and 14 pixels on mobile

devices. This size is generally considered to be a comfortable reading size for most users.

2. Headings: Make sure your headings are larger than your body text to create a clear visual hierarchy. A good rule of thumb is to have your main headings (H1) be at least twice the size of your body text, with subheadings (H2, H3, etc.) decreasing in size as their importance decreases.
3. Contrast: Ensure that there's enough contrast between your text and background colors, as this can significantly impact the readability of your content. The Web Content Accessibility Guidelines (WCAG) recommend a minimum contrast ratio of 4.5:1 for normal text and 3:1 for large text.

Now, let's move on to spacing. Spacing in UX design refers to the space between letters, words, lines, and paragraphs. Proper spacing is crucial for making your content easily digestible and ensuring that users can quickly scan and comprehend your information. Here are some key aspects of spacing to consider in your designs:

1. Letter-spacing: This refers to the space between individual characters in a word. To improve readability, it's essential to strike a balance between too tight and too loose letter-spacing. A good rule of thumb is to keep the default letter-spacing provided by the font you're using, as this is usually optimized for readability.
2. Word-spacing: This is the space between words in a line of text. The default word-spacing for most fonts is typically adequate, but you can adjust it slightly to improve readability if needed. Be cautious not to create too much or too little space

between words, as this can make the text difficult to read.

3. Line-spacing: Also known as leading, line-spacing is the space between lines of text in a paragraph. Adequate line-spacing is crucial for ensuring that your content is easy to read and doesn't appear cluttered. A good starting point for line-spacing is 1.4 to 1.6 times the font size, but this can vary depending on the specific font you're using.
4. Paragraph-spacing: This refers to the space between paragraphs in your content. Providing enough space between paragraphs can make it easier for users to differentiate between separate ideas and improve the overall readability of your content. A common approach is to use a space of around 1.5 to 2 times the line-spacing.

By thoughtfully considering font size and spacing in your designs, you can create a user experience that is accessible, easy to read, and enjoyable for a wide range of users. Remember to always test your designs with real users, including those with disabilities, to ensure that your choices meet the needs of your diverse audience.

In summary, proper font size and spacing play a crucial role in the readability and accessibility of digital content. By following the guidelines and best practices discussed in this section, you can make informed design decisions that benefit all users, regardless of their abilities or limitations. Keep in mind that your ultimate goal is to create a seamless user experience, where everyone can access, understand, and engage with your content comfortably.

To recap the key points of this section:

- Choose a font size that is legible and comfortable to read. Aim for a minimum of 16 pixels for body text

on desktop devices and 14 pixels on mobile devices.
- Use larger font sizes for headings, creating a clear visual hierarchy to guide users through your content.
- Ensure sufficient contrast between text and background colors to improve readability.
- Maintain balanced letter-spacing and word-spacing to make your content easy to read and understand.
- Adjust line-spacing and paragraph-spacing to create a comfortable reading experience and avoid cluttered text.

As you move forward in your UX design journey, always keep the principles of accessibility at the forefront of your decision-making process. By doing so, you'll not only meet the needs of a diverse audience, but you'll also create a more inclusive digital landscape that welcomes and supports everyone.

By mastering the art of font size and spacing, you'll be well-equipped to create user experiences that are not only visually appealing but also accessible to all. This, in turn, will lead to a more inclusive digital environment, where everyone can participate, learn, and thrive.

font size and spacing

When it comes to creating accessible designs, typography plays a crucial role. Font size and spacing are two key aspects of typography that can have a significant impact on the readability of your content. In this section, we'll explore the importance of font size and spacing, share guidelines and best practices, and provide tips to ensure your design is comfortable to read and easy to navigate for all users.

First, let's discuss the importance of font size. The size of your text can greatly affect the readability of your content. If your text is too small, users with visual impairments may struggle to read it. On the other hand, if your text is too large, it may become overwhelming and difficult to follow. Selecting an appropriate font size helps ensure that your content is legible and easy to read, regardless of your users' abilities or the devices they're using.

As a general guideline, it's recommended to use a base font size of at least 16 pixels for body text. Keep in mind that this is just a starting point; you may need to adjust the font size depending on the specific font you're using and your target audience's needs. For headings, choose a font size that's noticeably larger than your body text to create a clear visual hierarchy.

It's also essential to consider responsive design when choosing font sizes. Make sure your text remains legible and easy to read across different devices and screen sizes. This may involve adjusting font sizes and styles based on the device being used, as well as allowing users to resize text as needed.

Next, let's talk about spacing. Spacing plays a critical role in the readability and overall aesthetics of your design. Proper spacing between lines, paragraphs, and other elements can greatly improve the user experience.

Line spacing, also known as leading, is the space between lines of text. Insufficient line spacing can make it difficult for users to follow the text and may cause them to lose their place while reading. As a general rule, aim for a line-height of at least 1.5 times the font size. This provides enough space for users to read comfortably, without the lines of text feeling cramped or crowded.

Paragraph spacing is another important aspect to consider. Adding sufficient space between paragraphs can help break up large blocks of text, making it easier for users to follow the content and understand the structure of the document. A good practice is to use a space equivalent to 1.5 to 2 times the line-height between paragraphs.

Lastly, let's discuss letter-spacing, which refers to the space between individual characters. While most fonts are designed with optimal letter-spacing in mind, it may be necessary to adjust the spacing for certain fonts or users with specific needs, such as those with dyslexia. Slightly increasing letter-spacing can improve readability by reducing the likelihood of characters overlapping or appearing too close together.

Keep in mind that the guidelines provided in this section are just starting points. It's important to test your design with real users, including those with disabilities, to ensure your font size and spacing choices are effective and meet the needs of your audience.

To wrap up, font size and spacing are crucial elements of accessible design. By following these guidelines and best practices, you can help create a more readable and enjoyable experience for all users. Remember to consider the needs of your target audience and test your design with real users to ensure your choices are effective. By paying attention to these details, you'll be well on your way to creating more inclusive and accessible designs that everyone can enjoy.

Color contrast is another key aspect of accessible design, and it plays a significant role in the readability of text and the overall usability of a website or app. In this section, we'll explore the importance of color contrast, share guidelines for selecting appropriate color combinations, and provide tips for testing and improving the contrast of your designs.

The importance of color contrast cannot be overstated. For users with visual impairments, low-contrast text and elements can be difficult or even impossible to read. Additionally, low contrast can negatively impact the user experience for those without visual impairments, particularly when viewing content in less-than-ideal lighting conditions.

The Web Content Accessibility Guidelines (WCAG) provide recommendations for minimum contrast ratios for text and images of text. For normal-sized text (around 16px), the minimum contrast ratio is 4.5:1, while for larger text (typically 24px or 18px bold), the minimum ratio is 3:1. These ratios help ensure that your content is easily readable for users with various visual impairments, including color blindness and low vision.

When selecting colors for your design, consider not only the aesthetics but also the contrast ratios. You can use various online tools, such as color contrast checkers, to help you evaluate and select appropriate color combinations. These tools can calculate the contrast ratio between two colors and provide feedback on whether the combination meets the WCAG guidelines.

Beyond text, it's also essential to ensure that other elements, such as buttons, icons, and links, have sufficient contrast. For non-text elements, the WCAG guidelines recommend a minimum contrast ratio of 3:1. This helps ensure that important interactive elements are easy to see and interact with, particularly for users with visual impairments.

Testing your design with real users, including those with disabilities, is a crucial step in evaluating and improving color contrast. Users may provide valuable feedback on the legibility and usability of your design, helping you make any necessary adjustments.

In summary, color contrast is a vital element of accessible design. By following the WCAG guidelines for contrast ratios and using online tools to evaluate your color choices, you can create a more inclusive and accessible experience for all users. Remember to test your designs with real users and be prepared to make adjustments based on their feedback. By paying attention to color contrast, you'll be well on your way to creating designs that are not only visually appealing but also accessible to a diverse range of users.

contrast and color

Contrast and color: two essential ingredients in the recipe for accessible and visually appealing UX design. As designers, we have the responsibility to ensure that our digital creations are not only visually engaging but also easily navigable and accessible for all users, regardless of their abilities. In this section, we'll delve into the importance of contrast and color in UX design, and discuss some key principles and best practices for creating accessible and inclusive digital experiences.

Understanding the Importance of Contrast and Color

When it comes to designing user interfaces, contrast and color are fundamental elements that can significantly impact the usability and accessibility of a digital product. They help users distinguish between different elements on the page, enabling them to easily find, read, and interact with content.

For users with vision impairments, the effective use of contrast and color is even more crucial. High contrast between text and background colors can make content more legible, while using appropriate colors can reduce the risk of colorblind users encountering difficulties when navigating a website or app.

Contrast Ratio Guidelines

The Web Content Accessibility Guidelines (WCAG) provide specific recommendations for contrast ratios, which is the relative difference in brightness between text and background colors. According to WCAG 2.1, a minimum contrast ratio of 4.5:1 is required for normal text, while larger text (18 point or 14 point bold) should have a minimum contrast ratio of 3:1.

To help you meet these guidelines, there are numerous tools available online to measure contrast ratios, such as the WebAIM Color Contrast Checker. These tools make it easy to ensure that your designs adhere to accessibility standards and provide a better experience for users with visual impairments.

Color Selection and Colorblindness

When selecting colors for your designs, it's important to keep colorblind users in mind. Colorblindness affects approximately 1 in 12 men and 1 in 200 women worldwide. The most common form is red-green colorblindness, followed by blue-yellow colorblindness and total colorblindness.

To ensure that your designs are accessible to colorblind users, consider the following tips:

1. Use color combinations with high contrast: Opt for color combinations that can be easily distinguished by colorblind users, such as black and white, blue and yellow, or green and magenta.
2. Avoid problematic color combinations: Red and green, as well as blue and purple, can be difficult for some colorblind users to differentiate. Try to avoid these color combinations, or use them with caution.
3. Provide alternative cues: Use additional visual cues, such as patterns, textures, or icons, to help colorblind users understand the purpose of different interface elements.
4. Test your designs: Utilize tools like colorblindness simulators and accessibility checkers to ensure that your designs are usable and accessible for all users.

Accessible Color Palettes

Creating an accessible color palette is crucial for designing inclusive digital experiences. Here are some tips for building a color palette that meets accessibility standards:

1. Prioritize high-contrast colors: Include a range of colors with high contrast ratios in your palette to

ensure that text and interface elements are legible.
2. Keep it simple: A simple color palette with fewer colors can make it easier for users to understand and navigate your designs.
3. Use color to reinforce meaning: Use colors to provide additional context, such as using red for error messages or green for success messages.
4. Test your color palette: Use accessibility tools to ensure that your color palette meets WCAG guidelines and is accessible for users with various visual impairments.

In a Nutshell

Contrast and color play a vital role in creating accessible and inclusive UX designs. By understanding the importance of these elements and implementing best practices, we can create digital experiences that are visually engaging, easily navigable, and accessible for all users. As UX designers, our primary goal should be to remove barriers and create seamless experiences that cater to the diverse needs of our audience.

The Power of Contrast

Strong contrast helps users distinguish between different interface elements and improves the overall readability of your content. When working with contrast, keep the following tips in mind:

1. Use high contrast for important elements: Ensure that critical interface elements, such as buttons, links, and form fields, have sufficient contrast to stand out from the background and be easily identifiable.
2. Don't overlook smaller elements: Even small interface elements, like icons or labels, should have enough contrast to be legible and accessible.

3. Consider contrast in hover and focus states: When designing interactive elements, make sure that the contrast is maintained or even increased when users hover or focus on them.
4. Balance contrast with visual hierarchy: While it's essential to have sufficient contrast, you should also maintain a visual hierarchy in your design, using lower-contrast elements for secondary or tertiary information.

Color as a Communication Tool

Colors can evoke emotions, set the tone for your design, and convey information. When using color in your UX designs, consider the following strategies:

1. Use color to guide users: Apply color strategically to direct users' attention to essential elements and actions within your design.
2. Convey meaning through color: Color can be used to reinforce the meaning of interface elements, like using red for error messages or green for success notifications.
3. Be mindful of cultural differences: Colors can have different meanings in various cultures, so it's crucial to research your target audience and consider potential cultural implications when selecting colors.
4. Maintain consistency: Use a consistent color scheme across your entire digital product to create a cohesive and easily navigable user experience.

Incorporating effective contrast and color into your UX designs is a crucial aspect of creating accessible and inclusive digital experiences. By understanding the importance of these elements, implementing best practices, and using available tools to test your designs, you can ensure that your digital products cater to the diverse needs of your audience.

text alternatives and captions

In our digital world, we often rely on visuals to convey information and engage users. However, for individuals with vision impairments, these visuals can become barriers to accessing and enjoying the content you've created. As UX designers, it's our responsibility to ensure that our designs are inclusive and accessible to everyone, regardless of their abilities. One of the most effective ways to do this is by providing text alternatives and captions for visual elements within our designs.

In this section, we'll discuss the importance of text alternatives and captions, the various forms they can take, and best practices for implementing them in your UX designs.

Understanding Text Alternatives

Text alternatives, also known as alt text or alternative text, are textual descriptions of visual elements, such as images, icons, or other graphical elements, that can be used by assistive technologies like screen readers to convey the meaning of the visual content to users with vision impairments. By providing text alternatives, you allow these users to understand the context and purpose of the visuals within your design.

Creating Effective Text Alternatives

To create effective text alternatives, consider the following guidelines:

1. Be descriptive and concise: Text alternatives should accurately describe the visual content in a clear and concise manner. Avoid using overly complex language or lengthy descriptions.

2. Convey the purpose of the visual element: Make sure the text alternative explains the purpose of the visual element within the context of the page or application. This might include describing the action associated with an icon or button, the content of an infographic, or the subject of a photograph.
3. Avoid redundancy: If the visual element's purpose is already clearly described in the surrounding text, you might not need a text alternative. In these cases, use an empty alt attribute (e.g., alt="") to avoid duplicate information being read by assistive technologies.
4. Don't use "image of" or "graphic of": Assistive technologies already identify the element as an image, so there's no need to state this in the text alternative.

The Importance of Captions

Captions are another essential aspect of accessibility in UX design, especially for users with hearing impairments. Captions are text-based representations of the audio content within multimedia files, such as videos or audio clips, allowing users to read the spoken dialogue, sound effects, and music descriptions while consuming the media.

Implementing Captions in Your UX Designs

To ensure your multimedia content is accessible, consider these guidelines for implementing captions:

1. Use synchronized captions: Captions should be synchronized with the corresponding audio content, appearing on the screen at the same time as the spoken dialogue or sound effect they represent.

2. Ensure readability: Captions should be easy to read, with a sufficient font size, clear typeface, and high contrast between the text and background. Also, consider providing options for users to customize the appearance of captions to suit their needs.
3. Include sound effect and music descriptions: In addition to spoken dialogue, captions should include descriptions of significant sound effects and music to help users understand the context and atmosphere of the multimedia content.
4. Support multiple languages: If your target audience speaks multiple languages, consider providing captions in those languages to increase the accessibility of your content.

Incorporating text alternatives and captions into your UX designs might seem like a small detail, but for users with vision or hearing impairments, these elements can make all the difference in their ability to access and enjoy your content. By prioritizing accessibility and implementing these best practices, you're not only creating a more inclusive digital experience, but you're also enhancing your product's overall usability and user satisfaction.

As you continue your journey as a UX designer, always keep in mind the diverse needs of your users and strive to create designs that cater to everyone, regardless of their abilities. By incorporating text alternatives and captions into your designs, you're taking a significant step toward achieving this goal.

As a UX designer, it's essential to remember that incorporating text alternatives and captions is not a one-time effort; it's an ongoing commitment to inclusivity and accessibility. Continually reviewing and updating your designs to ensure they meet the needs of users with disabilities is a vital aspect of being a responsible and empathetic designer.

Further Considerations and Resources

As you continue to explore the world of accessibility in UX design, you may find additional resources and tools that can assist you in implementing text alternatives and captions effectively. Here are a few resources to consider:

1. Automated accessibility tools: Various automated tools can help you assess the accessibility of your designs, including the presence of text alternatives and captions. These tools can serve as a starting point for identifying areas that require improvement, but remember that they cannot replace manual testing and human judgment.
2. Collaboration with accessibility experts: Consult with accessibility experts, either within your organization or externally, to gain valuable insights and feedback on your designs. These professionals can provide guidance and recommendations for addressing accessibility challenges and ensuring compliance with relevant standards and guidelines.
3. User testing with diverse audiences: Conduct user testing with individuals who have different disabilities to gather first-hand feedback on the effectiveness of your text alternatives, captions, and overall design. This feedback can help you identify areas for improvement and further enhance the accessibility of your designs.

By incorporating text alternatives and captions in your designs and continually refining your accessibility practices, you're actively contributing to a more inclusive digital landscape. As a UX designer, your role in shaping accessible experiences is crucial, and by embracing these principles, you can help ensure that your designs are enjoyable and accessible to all users, regardless of their abilities.

6 / color and contrast accessibility

color theory and accessibility

COLOR PLAYS a significant role in the world of UX design, influencing how users perceive and interact with digital products. However, when it comes to accessibility, color choices can have an even more profound impact on users with various impairments. In this section, we'll explore the intersection of color theory and accessibility, highlighting best practices for choosing colors that enhance usability and inclusivity.

Understanding Color Theory

Before diving into the specifics of accessibility, let's first take a brief look at color theory. At its core, color theory is the study of how colors interact with one another and how they influence human perception and emotion. It involves the combination of color principles, such as the color wheel, color harmony, and color context, to create visually appealing and effective designs.

The color wheel is a visual representation of the relationships between colors, including primary, secondary, and tertiary colors. Color harmony refers to the balance and pleasing visual arrangement of colors, while color context describes how colors can change in appearance when placed next to other colors.

Now that we have a foundational understanding of color theory let's explore how it relates to accessibility in UX design.

Color Contrast

One of the most critical aspects of accessible design is ensuring sufficient color contrast between text and background elements. This is particularly important for users with visual impairments or color vision deficiencies, as low contrast can make content difficult or even impossible to read.

The Web Content Accessibility Guidelines (WCAG) provide specific recommendations for color contrast ratios to ensure readability for all users. For example, the minimum contrast ratio for normal-sized text is 4.5:1, while large text should have a contrast ratio of at least 3:1. By adhering to these guidelines, you can create designs that are more accessible to a wide range of users.

To check the contrast ratios of your color choices, consider using online tools like WebAIM's Color Contrast Checker, which can help you assess and adjust your designs as needed.

Color Combinations

Another aspect of color theory that's relevant to accessibility is the choice of color combinations. Some color combinations can be problematic for users with color vision deficiencies, such as red-green color blindness. To ensure that your designs are accessible to individuals with color vision impairments, try to avoid relying solely on color to convey information.

Instead, consider using additional visual cues, like patterns, icons, or labels, to ensure that users can understand and interact with your designs even if they cannot perceive certain colors. You can also use online tools like Coblis – the Color Blindness Simulator to see how your designs appear to users with various types of color blindness.

Color and Emotion

Color theory also delves into the emotional and psychological effects that colors can have on users. When considering accessibility, it's essential to keep these effects in mind, as they can influence the overall user experience.

For instance, certain colors can evoke specific emotions or associations (e.g., red for urgency or danger, blue for calmness and stability). While these associations can be useful in certain contexts, it's important to remember that they may not be universal, and different cultures or personal experiences can shape how users perceive colors.

Additionally, some users may have difficulty perceiving or processing overly stimulating visual environments, such as those with sensory processing disorders or cognitive impairments. In these cases, it's essential to strike a balance between using color to evoke emotion and maintaining a calm, accessible design that won't overwhelm users.

Tips for Accessible Color Design

With the principles of color theory and accessibility in mind, here are a few tips to help you create more inclusive designs:

1. Choose high-contrast color combinations for text and backgrounds.
2. Avoid relying solely on color to convey information.
3. Use additional visual cues, like patterns, icons, or labels, to supplement color choices.
4. Be mindful of cultural and personal differences in color perception and emotional associations.
5. Test your designs with color-blindness simulators and contrast-checking tools.
6. Opt for simple and clean color schemes that are easy to process and understand.

7. Consider the emotional impact of colors, but avoid overstimulation that could be problematic for users with sensory processing or cognitive impairments.
8. Keep accessibility in mind from the beginning of the design process to ensure that your color choices are inclusive and effective.

In Conclusion

When it comes to creating accessible and inclusive UX designs, the thoughtful application of color theory is essential. By understanding the principles of color theory and how they intersect with accessibility, designers can make informed decisions about color choices that enhance the overall user experience for individuals with various impairments.

From considering contrast ratios and color combinations to understanding the emotional impact of colors, designers must strike a balance between aesthetics and usability. By incorporating accessible design principles and testing your designs using available tools, you can create digital products that are not only visually appealing but also inclusive and usable by a diverse range of users.

In the end, your commitment to accessible color choices will not only benefit users with impairments but also improve the overall user experience for everyone, leading to more successful and satisfying digital products. So, as you continue your journey in UX design, remember the power of color theory and its role in creating accessible, inclusive, and engaging experiences for all.

choosing accessible color palettes

A key aspect of designing with accessibility in mind is selecting color palettes that cater to the needs of all users, including those with vision impairments. Color plays a vital role in UX design, as it influences user perception, brand identity, and overall experience. In this section, we will explore how to choose accessible color palettes to ensure that your designs are visually engaging and usable for a diverse range of users.

1. Understand the needs of your audience

Before you begin selecting colors for your palette, it's essential to have a clear understanding of your target audience and their needs. Consider the age, gender, cultural background, and potential impairments of your users. For instance, older adults may have difficulty distinguishing between certain colors, while colorblind users may struggle with specific color combinations. By keeping your audience's needs in mind, you can select colors that cater to their unique requirements.

1. Focus on contrast

One of the most critical aspects of accessible color palettes is ensuring adequate contrast between text and background colors. High contrast is essential for users with low vision or color vision deficiencies, as it makes text more legible and easier to read. When choosing colors, ensure that there is sufficient contrast between foreground and background elements. The Web Content Accessibility Guidelines (WCAG) recommend a minimum contrast ratio of 4.5:1 for standard text and 3:1 for large text.

1. Test your color choices

To guarantee that your color choices meet accessibility standards, it's crucial to test them using available tools. Online tools like the WebAIM Color Contrast Checker and the Color Safe tool can help you determine if your chosen colors meet the necessary contrast requirements. Additionally, consider using color-blindness simulators, such as Color Oracle or Coblis, to see how your designs appear to users with various forms of color vision deficiencies.

1. Consider color symbolism and cultural differences

Color carries various meanings and emotional associations, which can differ significantly depending on cultural background. To create accessible and inclusive designs, it's essential to consider the potential impact of color symbolism on your users. For instance, red may signify love or anger in some cultures, while in others, it can represent prosperity or good fortune. Research your target audience's cultural background and preferences to ensure that your color choices resonate positively with them.

1. Use color functionally and purposefully

In UX design, color should serve a functional purpose and not merely be used for decorative reasons. Color can be employed to indicate the hierarchy of information, guide users through the interface, and communicate essential information or feedback. When selecting colors for your palette, ensure that they support the user's goals and make the interface more intuitive and accessible.

1. Aim for simplicity

Complex color schemes can be overwhelming for users and may cause cognitive overload, particularly for those with cognitive impairments. To create accessible color palettes, opt for simplicity and minimalism. A limited color palette with a few well-chosen, contrasting colors can often be more effective and accessible than a complex, multi-hued scheme.

1. Be mindful of color combinations

Some color combinations can be problematic for users with color vision deficiencies, such as red-green or blue-yellow combinations. To create accessible color palettes, avoid using problematic color combinations in close proximity or for critical elements, such as text or call-to-action buttons. Instead, opt for color combinations that are easily distinguishable for users with various types of color vision deficiencies.

Selecting accessible color palettes is a crucial aspect of inclusive UX design. By understanding the needs of your target audience and the principles of accessible color selection, you can create designs that cater to a wide range of users, including those with vision impairments.

Remember to focus on contrast, test your color choices, consider color symbolism and cultural differences, use color functionally and purposefully, aim for simplicity, and be mindful of color combinations. By doing so, you'll create user experiences that are not only visually appealing but also accessible and inclusive for all.

By adopting accessible color palettes in your designs, you'll not only meet legal requirements and guidelines but also create a better overall user experience. Accessible design is good design, and as a UX designer, your goal should be to create products that are usable and enjoyable for everyone.

Incorporating accessibility into your design process from the outset can save you time and effort in the long run. It's much easier to make color choices that meet accessibility standards from the beginning rather than retrofitting an existing design that doesn't meet those requirements.

Finally, remember that accessibility is a continuous process. As you gain more experience and knowledge in UX design, you'll continue to refine and improve your ability to create accessible color palettes and design elements. Keep learning, experimenting, and iterating to ensure that your designs remain inclusive and accessible for all users.

With the right approach and commitment to accessibility, you can create designs that not only meet the diverse needs of your users but also elevate your brand reputation, expand market reach, and improve the overall user experience. By embracing accessible color palettes and design principles, you're well on your way to creating user experiences that truly benefit everyone.

ensuring sufficient contrast

Ensuring sufficient contrast is one of the cornerstones of accessible design. It ensures that users can easily distinguish between various elements on the screen, which is particularly important for people with low vision or color vision deficiencies. In this section, we'll discuss the importance of contrast, explain how to measure it, and provide tips on how to achieve sufficient contrast in your designs.

Why is contrast important in UX design?

Contrast is the difference in brightness and color between different elements on a screen. It helps users distinguish between text, images, and other visual components, making it easier to navigate and interact with the content. When contrast is insufficient, it becomes challenging for users, particularly those with vision impairments, to understand and use the interface effectively.

Consider the following scenarios:

1. A user with low vision trying to read small, light gray text on a slightly darker gray background.
2. A user with color vision deficiency struggling to differentiate between a red button and a green button with similar brightness levels.

In both cases, insufficient contrast can lead to confusion, frustration, and a negative user experience. By ensuring sufficient contrast in your designs, you'll create a more accessible and user-friendly experience for all.

Measuring contrast

To measure contrast, we use the contrast ratio, which is calculated by comparing the relative brightness of the lightest color (usually white) to the darkest color (usually black). The contrast ratio ranges from 1:1 (no contrast, e.g., white text on a white background) to 21:1 (maximum contrast, e.g., black text on a white background).

The Web Content Accessibility Guidelines (WCAG) provide specific contrast ratio recommendations for text and images of text:

1. Regular text: A minimum contrast ratio of 4.5:1.
2. Large text (18 points or larger, or 14 points and bold): A minimum contrast ratio of 3:1.

These guidelines apply to both solid and outlined text, as well as to text that appears on top of images or gradients.

There are various online tools available to help you measure contrast ratios, such as the WebAIM Color Contrast Checker and the Paciello Group's Colour Contrast Analyser. These tools can be invaluable in helping you ensure that your designs meet the recommended contrast ratios.

Tips for achieving sufficient contrast

1. Use high-contrast color combinations: Choose color pairs with high contrast ratios, such as black text on a white background, or white text on a dark background. Avoid using colors with similar brightness levels, as they can be difficult to differentiate for users with low vision or color vision deficiencies.

2. Utilize typography effectively: Choose clear, legible fonts with good spacing and weight. Avoid thin or decorative fonts that may be difficult to read, especially at smaller sizes.
3. Be mindful of text over images or gradients: When placing text over images or gradients, ensure that the contrast between the text and the background remains sufficient. You can achieve this by adding a background color or shadow behind the text, or by adjusting the image or gradient itself to provide better contrast.
4. Consider contrast in other interface elements: Contrast is essential not only for text but also for other interface elements, such as buttons, icons, and form fields. Ensure that these elements have sufficient contrast with their backgrounds and with each other to make them easy to see and interact with.
5. Test your designs with real users: To ensure that your designs are accessible, test them with users who have a range of vision abilities. This will help you identify and address any contrast issues that you may not have noticed otherwise.

In conclusion, ensuring sufficient contrast in your designs is a crucial aspect of creating accessible and inclusive user experiences. By understanding the importance of contrast, measuring it accurately, and applying the tips provided in this section, you can create designs that cater to a wide range of users, including those with vision impairments and color vision deficiencies.

1. Use color-blindness simulators: To better understand how your designs may appear to users with color vision deficiencies, use color-blindness

simulators, such as the Color Oracle or Toptal Color Blind Filter. These tools can help you identify potential contrast issues and make adjustments accordingly.

2. Focus on hierarchy: A well-defined visual hierarchy can help users quickly understand the structure and relationships between different elements on a page. Use contrast to create a clear hierarchy, with the most important elements having the highest contrast.
3. Implement accessible hover and focus states: Ensure that interactive elements, such as buttons and links, have sufficient contrast when hovered or focused. This will help users with motor impairments and those who rely on keyboard navigation to understand which elements are interactive and their current state.
4. Leverage accessible design systems: Many design systems, such as Google's Material Design or IBM's Carbon Design System, already incorporate accessible contrast levels in their color palettes and components. Leveraging these design systems can help you create accessible interfaces with less effort.
5. Keep learning and iterating: Accessibility is an ongoing process, and as you gain more experience, your understanding of contrast and its role in accessible design will continue to grow. Continuously seek feedback from users and experts, and use that feedback to improve your designs.

By embracing these tips and incorporating them into your design process, you'll be well on your way to creating accessible and inclusive user experiences. The importance of contrast in design cannot be overstated, as it directly impacts users' ability to perceive, understand, and engage with digital content.

tools and techniques for evaluating color accessibility

Evaluating color accessibility is a vital part of creating inclusive and accessible designs. Thankfully, there are many tools and techniques available to help designers and developers ensure their color choices meet accessibility guidelines and provide a positive experience for all users. In this section, we'll explore some of these tools and techniques, and share tips on how to effectively use them in your design process.

1. Color contrast checkers

One of the most straightforward methods for evaluating color accessibility is using a color contrast checker. These tools compare the contrast ratio between two colors to determine if they meet the Web Content Accessibility Guidelines (WCAG) criteria for text and background color combinations. Some popular color contrast checkers include:

- WebAIM's Color Contrast Checker
- Lea Verou's Contrast Ratio
- Colorable by Brent Jackson

To use these tools, simply input the foreground and background colors you're working with, and the tool will tell you if the contrast ratio meets the required accessibility standards.

1. Browser extensions

Browser extensions can help you evaluate color accessibility in real-time, directly within your web browser. These extensions can highlight potential contrast issues and provide recommendations for improving accessibility. Some popular browser extensions for color accessibility include:

- Accessibility Insights for Web: This extension offers a comprehensive set of accessibility tools, including a color contrast analyzer.
- WCAG Color Contrast Checker: A simple extension focused on evaluating color contrast ratios.

1. Design tools with built-in accessibility features

Many modern design tools, such as Adobe XD, Sketch, and Figma, now include built-in accessibility features that can help you evaluate color choices as you design. These features can provide real-time feedback on color contrast ratios and offer suggestions for more accessible alternatives. Be sure to explore the accessibility features within your preferred design tool and incorporate them into your workflow.

1. Color blindness simulators

Color blindness simulators can help you understand how your designs may appear to users with color vision deficiencies. By simulating various forms of color blindness, you can identify potential issues and make adjustments to ensure your designs remain accessible. Some popular color blindness simulators include:

- Color Oracle: A free color blindness simulator available for Windows, macOS, and Linux.
- Toptal Color Blind Filter: An online tool that allows you to simulate various types of color blindness on your designs.

1. Manual testing with real users

While automated tools can provide valuable insights, there's no substitute for feedback from real users. Include users with different types of disabilities, including those with color vision deficiencies, in your usability testing process. This will allow you to gather valuable feedback on your designs and identify potential accessibility issues that might not be detected by automated tools.

1. Accessible design systems and color palettes

Leveraging pre-made accessible design systems and color palettes can help streamline your design process while ensuring your color choices meet accessibility standards. Some popular accessible design systems include:

- Google's Material Design
- IBM's Carbon Design System
- Microsoft's Fluent Design System

These design systems provide accessible color palettes, components, and guidance on creating inclusive designs that meet accessibility requirements.

1. Online courses and resources

To further hone your skills in color accessibility, consider taking online courses or attending workshops on the topic. Many reputable organizations and experts in the field offer training on accessibility, including color theory and accessibility best practices. Additionally, there are countless articles, blog posts, and resources available to deepen your understanding of color accessibility and how to effectively implement it in your designs.

By integrating these tools and techniques into your design process, you'll be better equipped to create accessible and inclusive user experiences. Evaluating color accessibility is not just a matter of compliance with legal requirements; it's about designing with empathy and understanding, ensuring that all users can enjoy and engage with your digital content.

By making a commitment to color accessibility and incorporating these tools and techniques into your workflow, you'll be able to create designs that are not only visually appealing but also accessible to a wider audience. This inclusive approach benefits both your users and your brand, as it demonstrates your commitment to providing a positive experience for all.

7 / accessible navigation and interaction

keyboard accessibility

KEYBOARD ACCESSIBILITY IS a critical aspect of creating an inclusive user experience. When designing digital products, it's important to ensure that users can interact with your content and navigate your interface using only their keyboard. Many individuals, including those with motor impairments or visual impairments, rely on keyboard navigation as their primary means of interacting with digital interfaces. In this section, we will explore the importance of keyboard accessibility, as well as practical tips and best practices for implementing it in your designs.

First, let's discuss the reasons why keyboard accessibility is essential. For users with motor impairments, using a mouse or touch screen may be difficult or impossible. These individuals often rely on alternative input methods, such as keyboard navigation, to interact with digital content. Additionally, individuals with visual impairments often use screen readers, which are software applications that convert text to speech or Braille. Screen reader users typically navigate web pages and applications using keyboard commands. Ensuring keyboard accessibility is a crucial part of creating an inclusive and accessible user experience for these individuals.

To create a keyboard-accessible interface, you need to be mindful of several key design elements. Here are some essential principles to guide your efforts:

1. Focus indicators: When users navigate your interface using their keyboard, it's vital that they can easily see which element currently has focus. Ensure that you provide clear visual indicators for the focused element, such as a distinct outline or a change in background color. This allows users to track their progress through your interface easily and confidently.
2. Logical tab order: When users navigate using the 'Tab' key, they expect the focus to move through elements in a logical and predictable order. This typically means following the visual layout of the page or application, moving from left to right and top to bottom. To create a logical tab order, ensure that your HTML markup is structured appropriately, and use the 'tabindex' attribute to control the order when necessary.
3. Accessible controls: Make sure that all interactive elements in your design, such as buttons, links, and form fields, can be easily accessed and activated using the keyboard. This includes providing alternative methods for activating custom controls, such as using the 'Enter' or 'Space' key to trigger a button. Also, be sure to include appropriate labels and instructions for form fields, so users understand how to interact with them using only their keyboard.
4. Keyboard shortcuts: Consider providing keyboard shortcuts for frequently used actions, as they can

significantly improve efficiency and productivity for keyboard users. When implementing shortcuts, ensure that they are clearly communicated to the user and do not conflict with existing keyboard commands used by the operating system or assistive technologies.

5. Avoid keyboard traps: A keyboard trap occurs when a user is unable to navigate away from a particular element using the keyboard. This can be incredibly frustrating and create an inaccessible experience. To avoid keyboard traps, ensure that users can always move focus away from an element using standard keyboard commands, such as 'Tab' or 'Shift + Tab.'
6. Testing: As with any aspect of accessibility, testing is a crucial part of ensuring that your designs are keyboard-accessible. Test your interface using only your keyboard to navigate and interact with elements. This will help you identify any issues or areas for improvement, and ensure that your design is accessible to keyboard users.

Implementing these principles will help you create an interface that is accessible and inclusive for keyboard users. By doing so, you're not only meeting the needs of individuals with disabilities but also improving the overall user experience for all users. Keyboard accessibility benefits everyone, as it provides an alternative method of interaction that can be more efficient and precise in certain situations.

In the world of digital design, accessibility should always be a top priority. By embracing keyboard accessibility and incorporating it into your design process, you'll be taking a significant step toward creating a more inclusive and user-friendly experience for everyone. It's important to remember that creating accessible products doesn't mean sacrificing aesthetics or functionality. In fact, designing with accessibility in mind often leads to cleaner, more intuitive interfaces that are easier for everyone to use.

To further improve your understanding of keyboard accessibility, consider exploring the following resources:

1. Web Content Accessibility Guidelines (WCAG): The WCAG provides comprehensive guidelines and success criteria for creating accessible digital content, including specific recommendations for keyboard accessibility.
2. ARIA (Accessible Rich Internet Applications) specification: ARIA is a set of attributes that can be added to HTML elements to improve their accessibility, particularly for users of assistive technologies. ARIA can be helpful in ensuring that custom controls and complex user interface components are accessible via keyboard navigation.
3. Online tutorials and courses: There are numerous online resources available to help you learn more about keyboard accessibility and how to implement it in your designs. Look for tutorials and courses that cover keyboard accessibility best practices, as well as hands-on examples and exercises.
4. Community and expert resources: Engage with the accessibility community by participating in online forums, attending conferences and meetups, and following accessibility experts on social media. This will help you stay up-to-date on the latest developments in the field, as well as provide opportunities to learn from the experiences of others.

As you continue to develop your skills in keyboard accessibility, it's important to remember that accessibility is an ongoing process. Be prepared to iterate on your designs and make improvements as you learn more and receive feedback from users. By continually striving to create more accessible and inclusive experiences, you'll not only be making a positive impact on the lives of individuals with disabilities but also contributing to a more inclusive digital landscape for everyone.

In summary, keyboard accessibility is an essential aspect of creating inclusive user experiences. By implementing the principles outlined in this section, you can ensure that your designs are accessible to a wider range of users, including those with motor and visual impairments.

focus management

Focus management is a crucial aspect of user experience design that ensures users can efficiently navigate and interact with a digital product. When done correctly, it helps users understand where they are on a page, what actions they can take, and how to complete their intended tasks. In this section, we'll explore what focus management entails, why it's essential for accessibility, and how to implement effective focus management techniques in your designs.

What is Focus Management?

Focus management refers to the process of controlling which user interface elements receive input and attention at any given time. In the context of digital products, focus management typically involves handling keyboard navigation and ensuring that users can move between interactive elements such as buttons, links, and form inputs in a logical and predictable manner.

Why is Focus Management Important for Accessibility?

Effective focus management is especially important for users with disabilities, as it helps them navigate and interact with digital products more easily. For example, individuals with motor impairments may rely on keyboards or other input devices instead of a mouse, making proper focus management essential for their experience. Similarly, users with visual impairments may use screen readers that rely on focus to read and interact with content.

Implementing Focus Management Techniques

Here are some fundamental techniques to ensure effective focus management in your designs:

1. Logical tab order: When users navigate through your website or application using the Tab key, the order in which interactive elements receive focus should be logical and predictable. This typically means following the natural reading order—left to right, top to bottom—for left-to-right languages. To achieve a logical tab order, arrange your HTML code accordingly and use the tabindex attribute only when necessary.
2. Visible focus indicators: When an element has focus, it should be visually apparent to the user. This can be achieved by applying a distinct style to the focused element, such as an outline, border, or background color change. Make sure the focus indicator is noticeable and has sufficient contrast with the surrounding elements.
3. Skip navigation links: For users who rely on keyboard navigation, having to tab through a large number of elements before reaching the main content can be frustrating. By providing skip navigation links at the beginning of your page, you can enable users to bypass repetitive elements such as headers and menus, allowing them to access the primary content more quickly.
4. Managing focus in modal dialogs: When a modal dialog appears, the focus should be trapped within

the dialog to prevent users from accidentally interacting with elements in the background. Ensure that the focus moves to the first focusable element within the modal and cycles back to the last focusable element when the user reaches the end.

5. Avoid focus traps: A focus trap occurs when a user's focus gets stuck on a particular element or group of elements, preventing them from navigating away using the keyboard. To avoid focus traps, make sure all interactive elements are part of the natural tab order, and avoid using tabindex values greater than 0.
6. Use ARIA roles and landmarks: ARIA roles and landmarks help convey the structure of your content to users of assistive technologies. By using appropriate ARIA roles and landmarks, you can make it easier for users to navigate your content and understand the relationships between different elements.

Testing and Improving Focus Management

Once you have implemented focus management techniques in your designs, it's essential to test your work to ensure it functions as intended. Here are some tips for testing focus management:

1. Use keyboard navigation: Navigate through your digital product using only the keyboard to ensure the tab order is logical, focus indicators are visible, and there are no focus traps.
2. Test with screen readers: Test your digital product with popular screen readers such as NVDA, JAWS, and VoiceOver to ensure that focus management works well for users who rely on these assistive technologies.

3. Seek feedback from users with disabilities: Engage users with various disabilities in the testing process to get their insights on how well your focus management techniques are working. This will help you identify any potential issues and areas for improvement that you may have missed during your own testing.
4. Use automated testing tools: Several automated testing tools can help you identify focus management issues. These tools, such as axe or Lighthouse, can quickly assess your digital product for accessibility problems and provide suggestions for improvements.
5. Regularly update and maintain your focus management: As your digital product evolves and new features are added, it's crucial to maintain and update your focus management strategies. This ensures that your focus management remains effective and continues to provide a positive user experience for all users, including those with disabilities.

Focus management is a key aspect of accessible user experience design, enabling users with disabilities to navigate and interact with digital products more easily. By implementing logical tab order, visible focus indicators, skip navigation links, and proper focus handling in modal dialogs, you can make your digital product more accessible and user-friendly. Testing your focus management techniques with keyboard navigation, screen readers, and user feedback will help you identify and address any issues and ensure a positive experience for all users.

accessible menus and navigation patterns

Navigating your way through a digital product should be a straightforward and enjoyable experience for all users. For those with disabilities, however, challenges may arise when trying to make sense of complex menus and navigation patterns. In this section, we'll explore how to create accessible menus and navigation patterns that cater to a diverse range of users, ensuring that everyone has the opportunity to enjoy your digital product to the fullest.

The Importance of Accessible Menus and Navigation

When designing a digital product, it's essential to prioritize accessibility, as it allows users with disabilities to navigate and interact with the product more easily. Accessible menus and navigation patterns can help users with visual, cognitive, and motor impairments understand the structure of your product and move between different sections with ease.

Creating Accessible Menus

Menus are a crucial element of any digital product, helping users find the information they need and make decisions. Here are some tips to create accessible menus:

1. Keep it simple: A clean and straightforward menu design makes it easier for users to understand the options and make choices. Avoid complex menu structures, and limit the number of menu items to reduce cognitive overload.
2. Use clear labels: Make sure your menu items have descriptive and concise labels, so users know what to expect when they click on them. Avoid using ambiguous or generic terms that may be confusing.
3. Make menus keyboard accessible: Ensure that all menu items can be accessed using the keyboard alone. This helps users with motor impairments or those who rely on keyboard navigation.

4. Provide visible focus indicators: When a user navigates through the menu using a keyboard, make sure the currently focused item is clearly highlighted. This helps users with visual impairments understand their current position within the menu.
5. Ensure proper contrast: Use colors with sufficient contrast for menu items and their background to make the menu easily readable for users with visual impairments.
6. Offer multiple ways to navigate: For digital products with extensive content, consider providing additional ways for users to navigate, such as a search bar or a site map.

Designing Accessible Navigation Patterns

In addition to accessible menus, it's essential to create accessible navigation patterns. Here are some guidelines to follow:

1. Consistent navigation: Maintain a consistent navigation structure throughout your digital product. Consistency helps users build a mental model of your product's layout, making it easier for them to navigate and find information.
2. Logical order: Arrange navigation elements in a logical order that reflects the importance and relationships between sections. This helps users with cognitive impairments understand your product's structure and move between sections more efficiently.
3. Use descriptive links: Ensure that all links have clear and informative text that describes the destination or the action that will be taken when

the link is clicked. Avoid using vague phrases like "click here" or "learn more."

4. Include ARIA landmarks: Use ARIA landmarks to label the different sections of your digital product, such as navigation, main content, and footer. This helps screen reader users understand the layout and more easily navigate through the content.
5. Responsive design: Make sure your navigation patterns work well on various devices and screen sizes. This ensures that users with different devices or assistive technologies can access and navigate your digital product comfortably.

Testing and Refining Your Accessible Menus and Navigation Patterns

To ensure your menus and navigation patterns are truly accessible, it's essential to test them thoroughly. Here are some strategies for testing:

1. Keyboard navigation: Test your digital product using only a keyboard to ensure all menu items and navigation elements can be reached and activated.
2. Screen reader testing: Use a screen reader to test your digital product and listen to how the menus and navigation patterns are announced.
3. Test with real users: Conduct usability testing with users with various disabilities to gain valuable insights into how they navigate and interact with your digital product. This feedback can help you identify areas for improvement and make necessary adjustments.
4. Use automated tools: Utilize accessibility testing tools to help identify issues with your menus and navigation patterns. These tools can provide a helpful starting point, but remember that manual

testing and user feedback are also vital to ensure a truly accessible experience.

5. Review WCAG guidelines: Consult the Web Content Accessibility Guidelines (WCAG) to ensure your menus and navigation patterns meet the recommended standards. The guidelines provide a comprehensive framework to help you create accessible digital products.

designing accessible forms and controls

Imagine trying to fill out a form online, only to realize that it's confusing, difficult to navigate, or even impossible to use. For people with disabilities, this can be an all too common experience. As designers, it's our responsibility to ensure that the digital products we create are accessible to all users, including those with disabilities. In this section, we'll discuss the importance of designing accessible forms and controls and offer practical tips to help you create a more inclusive experience.

The Importance of Accessible Forms and Controls

Forms are a fundamental component of many digital products, allowing users to submit information, sign up for services, make purchases, and more. However, if a form is not designed with accessibility in mind, it can create significant barriers for users with disabilities. Accessible forms and controls help ensure that everyone, regardless of their abilities, can interact with your digital product and complete essential tasks with ease.

Tips for Designing Accessible Forms and Controls

1. Label elements clearly: Each form control, such as text input fields, checkboxes, and radio buttons, should have a clear and concise label. Screen reader users rely on these labels to understand the purpose of each control. Use the 'for' attribute in the

label element to associate it with the corresponding form control, ensuring that the label is programmatically linked to the control.

2. Use fieldsets and legends: When you have a group of related form controls, such as a set of radio buttons, use the 'fieldset' element to group them together and the 'legend' element to provide a descriptive label for the group. This structure helps screen reader users understand the relationship between the form controls and the context in which they should be used.
3. Provide helpful error messages: When users encounter errors while filling out a form, it's crucial to provide clear and informative error messages that help them understand and correct the problem. Ensure that error messages are announced to screen reader users and are visually distinct for users with low vision. Additionally, consider providing real-time validation to help users identify and fix errors as they occur.
4. Offer clear instructions: When a form requires users to input information in a specific format or follow certain guidelines, provide clear and concise instructions to help them understand the requirements. Place these instructions near the relevant form controls so users can easily access them when needed.
5. Ensure keyboard accessibility: Users with motor impairments often rely on keyboard navigation, so it's essential to make sure your forms and controls are accessible using only the keyboard. Test your form to ensure that all form controls can be accessed and manipulated using the 'Tab' key and other standard keyboard commands.

6. Design with touch devices in mind: Many users interact with digital products using touch devices, such as smartphones and tablets. Ensure that form controls are large enough to be easily tapped, and provide sufficient spacing between controls to prevent accidental selections.
7. Don't rely solely on color: Using color alone to indicate required fields, errors, or other important information can be problematic for users with color vision deficiencies. Supplement color cues with text, icons, or other visual indicators to ensure that all users can understand the information being conveyed.
8. Implement accessible CAPTCHAs: CAPTCHAs can be particularly challenging for users with disabilities, especially those with visual impairments. If you need to include a CAPTCHA on your form, consider using accessible alternatives, such as audio CAPTCHAs or logic-based questions.
9. Use ARIA attributes where necessary: The Accessible Rich Internet Applications (ARIA) specification provides a way to make web content and applications more accessible to people with disabilities. Use ARIA attributes, such as 'aria-required' and 'aria-describedby', to provide additional context and information for screen reader users when standard HTML elements don't suffice.
10. Design for screen magnification: Users with low vision often rely on screen magnification tools to enlarge content and make it easier to read. Ensure that your forms and controls remain usable and legible when magnified, and avoid using fixed font sizes or layouts that may break when zoomed in.

11. Optimize for speech input: Some users may interact with your digital product using speech input, such as voice recognition software. Design your forms and controls to be compatible with speech input by using clear and concise labels, and avoid using visual cues that are difficult for speech input users to describe.
12. Provide alternatives to time-sensitive actions: If your form includes time-sensitive actions, such as a timed quiz or a session timeout, ensure that users with disabilities have sufficient time to complete the task. Provide alternatives, such as the ability to request additional time or disable the time limit, to accommodate users who may require more time due to their disabilities.
13. Test with real users: While following best practices and guidelines is essential, there's no substitute for testing your forms and controls with real users, including those with disabilities. Conduct usability testing with a diverse group of users to identify any potential accessibility issues and gather valuable feedback to improve your design.

Designing accessible forms and controls is a crucial aspect of creating a digital product that is inclusive and usable for everyone.

8 / accessible multimedia content

image accessibility (alt text, long descriptions)

WHEN IT COMES to creating an accessible digital experience, the proper use of images plays a significant role. Images can enhance the content and help to convey complex ideas more effectively. However, to make sure that everyone can benefit from the visuals on your website or app, you must consider accessibility. In this section, we'll explore how to make images more accessible using alternative text (alt text) and long descriptions, as well as some best practices to follow.

1. Understanding the importance of image accessibility: For users with visual impairments or those who rely on screen readers, images can pose a barrier to understanding content. By providing alternative ways to access the information presented in images, you can ensure that all users can fully experience and understand your digital product.

2. Alt text – a brief overview: Alt text is a short, descriptive text that conveys the essential information or purpose of an image for users who cannot see it. Screen readers read the alt text aloud, allowing visually impaired users to understand the context and meaning of the image.
3. Writing effective alt text: When crafting alt text, aim for clarity and brevity. Describe the image's content or function in a succinct manner, ensuring that the description is informative and relevant to the surrounding content. Here are some tips for writing effective alt text:
4. Be specific: Describe the image's main subject or purpose.
5. Be concise: Keep the description brief, ideally under 125 characters.
6. Avoid redundancy: Don't include phrases like "image of" or "picture of" in the alt text, as screen readers already announce the presence of an image.
7. Stay relevant: Ensure the alt text contributes to the overall understanding of the content.
8. When to use empty alt text: In some cases, an image may be purely decorative and not contribute any additional information to the content. In these instances, you can use empty alt text (alt="") to indicate to screen readers that the image can be skipped. This prevents users from hearing unnecessary or repetitive information.
9. Long descriptions for complex images: When an image contains a large amount of information, such as a chart, graph, or detailed illustration, a short alt text may not be sufficient to convey the image's content fully. In these cases, consider providing a long description that elaborates on the image's content in more detail. You can either include the

long description on the page near the image or provide a link to a separate page containing the description.

10. Best practices for long descriptions:
11. Be comprehensive: Ensure that the long description covers all the essential information presented in the image.
12. Use clear language: Make the description easy to understand, using plain language and avoiding jargon.
13. Structure the information: Organize the description logically, using headings and lists when appropriate.
14. Provide context: Explain how the image relates to the surrounding content and why it's important.
15. Implementing long descriptions: There are several ways to provide long descriptions for complex images:
16. Use the 'aria-describedby' attribute: This ARIA attribute associates the image with a specific element containing the long description.
17. Include a link to the long description: Place a link near the image that directs users to a separate page or section with the long description.
18. Utilize a caption or nearby text: You can also include the long description within a caption or as part of the surrounding text.
19. Testing image accessibility: As with any other aspect of accessibility, it's essential to test your images to ensure they are accessible to all users. This includes checking that the alt text and long descriptions are present and accurate, and ensuring that screen readers can access the information correctly.

20. Additional image accessibility considerations: Besides alt text and long descriptions, there are other factors to consider when making your images accessible:
21. Use high-quality images: Ensure that your images are clear and sharp to accommodate users with low vision.
22. Avoid relying solely on color: Some users may have difficulty distinguishing certain colors. Make sure the information in your images can be understood even if the colors aren't perceivable.
23. Opt for simple and clean designs: Overly complicated images can be challenging to understand for users with cognitive disabilities. Strive for clear, straightforward visuals.
24. Scalable vector graphics (SVGs): When possible, use SVGs for graphics and icons. SVGs are resolution-independent, meaning they can be scaled without losing quality. This makes them ideal for users who may need to zoom in on images for better visibility.
25. Accessible image maps: Image maps are clickable areas on an image that link to different destinations. To make image maps accessible, add appropriate alt text for each clickable area, and ensure that the image map is keyboard-navigable.
26. Captions for multimedia content: When using images within videos or other multimedia content, consider providing captions that describe the visual elements for users who cannot see them. This helps ensure that all users can follow along with the content, regardless of their ability to see the images.

By taking the time to implement these image accessibility strategies, you're creating a more inclusive environment for your users. Accessible images not only benefit those with disabilities but can also improve the overall user experience for everyone.

video and audio accessibility (captions, transcripts, audio descriptions)

Welcome to the section on video and audio accessibility! In this section, we'll dive into the importance of making multimedia content accessible to users with various disabilities. We'll explore the essential techniques, such as captions, transcripts, and audio descriptions, and how they contribute to creating an inclusive and user-friendly digital experience.

1. The importance of accessible multimedia: Videos and audio content have become increasingly popular on the web, especially in the age of social media and online learning platforms. For individuals with disabilities, it's crucial to provide accessible alternatives to these multimedia elements, ensuring that they can access and enjoy the content as seamlessly as possible.
2. Captions: Captions are text versions of the spoken dialogue and relevant sound effects in a video. They are synchronized with the video, allowing users who are deaf or hard of hearing to follow along with the content. Captions should be accurate, complete, and properly timed to ensure that users can understand the context of the video without any confusion.
3. Closed captions vs. open captions: Closed captions can be toggled on and off by the user, while open captions are permanently visible and cannot be turned off. When creating captions for your videos, consider providing closed captions as they offer

more flexibility for users who may not need or want them.

4. Transcripts: Transcripts are text versions of the spoken content in a video or audio file, typically provided as a separate document. Transcripts are particularly useful for users who are deaf or hard of hearing, as well as users who may have a cognitive disability or prefer to read the content rather than watch or listen to it.
5. Interactive transcripts: An interactive transcript is a dynamic version of a traditional transcript that allows users to click on a specific section of text to jump to that point in the video. This can be an excellent addition to your multimedia content, as it provides an additional layer of accessibility and interactivity.
6. Audio descriptions: Audio descriptions provide a spoken narration of the visual elements in a video, describing important actions, gestures, and scene changes for users who are blind or visually impaired. These descriptions are usually available as a separate audio track that can be toggled on and off by the user.
7. Implementing captions, transcripts, and audio descriptions: When creating accessible multimedia content, it's essential to consider the following best practices:
8. Synchronize your captions and audio descriptions with the video: Ensure that your captions and audio descriptions are properly timed to match the video content.
9. Use clear, concise language: Keep your captions and audio descriptions simple and easy to understand.

10. Test your multimedia content: Validate the accessibility of your multimedia content by testing it with actual users or using automated accessibility testing tools.
11. Video and audio player accessibility: The video or audio player you use to deliver your multimedia content should also be accessible to users with disabilities. Some features to look for in an accessible media player include:
12. Keyboard accessibility: Ensure that your media player can be fully controlled using only the keyboard.
13. Accessible controls: Provide clear, visible, and accessible controls for play, pause, volume, captions, and other features.
14. Customizable settings: Allow users to adjust settings, such as caption font size and color, to meet their specific needs.
15. Legal requirements: In many countries, there are legal requirements for providing accessible multimedia content. These laws often mandate the use of captions, transcripts, and audio descriptions for videos and audio files. Familiarize yourself with the accessibility laws and guidelines in your region to ensure compliance and avoid potential legal issues.
16. Tools for creating accessible multimedia content: There are various tools available to help you create captions, transcripts, and audio descriptions for your multimedia content. Some of these tools include:
17. Automatic captioning services: These services use speech recognition technology to generate captions for your videos. While they can be a helpful

starting point, it's essential to review and edit the generated captions for accuracy and completeness.

18. Professional captioning and transcription services: You can also hire professional services to create captions and transcripts for your multimedia content, ensuring high-quality and accurate results.
19. Audio description creation tools: There are software tools and services available that can help you create audio descriptions for your videos, either by using text-to-speech technology or by providing a platform for recording your own descriptions.
20. Tips for creating high-quality captions, transcripts, and audio descriptions:
21. Be accurate: Ensure that your captions, transcripts, and audio descriptions accurately represent the spoken and visual content in your multimedia files.
22. Use proper punctuation and grammar: Correct punctuation and grammar can make your captions and transcripts easier to read and understand.
23. Avoid jargon and abbreviations: Use clear, straightforward language to make your captions, transcripts, and audio descriptions accessible to users with varying levels of language proficiency or cognitive abilities.
24. Consider the timing: Ensure that your captions and audio descriptions are well-timed, allowing users to follow along with the content comfortably.
25. Continuous improvement: As with any aspect of accessibility, it's essential to continually evaluate and improve your multimedia content. Regularly review your captions, transcripts, and audio descriptions for accuracy and completeness, and be open to feedback from users who may have suggestions for improvement.

accessible animations and interactive elements

Creating an inclusive and accessible digital experience involves more than just considering the visual and auditory aspects of your content. Animations and interactive elements are increasingly common on websites and applications, and they bring unique accessibility challenges that must be addressed. This section will delve into the best practices for designing accessible animations and interactive elements, ensuring a positive experience for all users, regardless of their abilities or preferences.

1. Understanding the impact of animations: While animations can make a website or application more visually appealing and engaging, they can also create accessibility barriers for users with certain disabilities. For example, animations can cause dizziness or nausea for individuals with vestibular disorders, or they can be distracting for users with attention deficit disorders. Therefore, it's essential to consider the potential impact of animations on your users and design them with accessibility in mind.
2. Providing options to control animations: One way to make animations accessible is to provide users with the option to control their playback. This can include offering options to pause, slow down, or disable animations altogether. This allows users to customize their experience according to their preferences and abilities, ensuring that animations do not create barriers to accessing your content.
3. Avoiding content that could trigger seizures: It is crucial to ensure that your animations and interactive elements do not contain content that

could trigger seizures in individuals with photosensitive epilepsy. Avoid using rapidly flashing or flickering content, and ensure that any animations follow the guidelines set forth by the Web Content Accessibility Guidelines (WCAG) to minimize the risk of causing seizures.

4. Designing accessible interactive elements: Interactive elements, such as buttons, sliders, and dropdown menus, should be designed with accessibility in mind. This includes ensuring that interactive elements are:
5. Clearly labeled: Use descriptive labels and tooltips to help users understand the purpose and function of each interactive element.
6. Easily accessible: Ensure that interactive elements are easy to access using both a mouse and a keyboard, and that they are compatible with screen reader technology.
7. Visually distinct: Use clear visual cues, such as contrasting colors, borders, or hover effects, to help users identify interactive elements on the page.
8. Implementing focus indicators: To help users navigate your website or application using a keyboard, it is essential to implement focus indicators that clearly show which interactive element is currently selected. Ensure that focus indicators are visually distinct and easy to see, and that they follow a logical order when users navigate through your content.
9. Testing and refining interactive elements: As with any aspect of accessibility, it's essential to test your interactive elements and animations to ensure that they are accessible to users with different abilities and preferences. This can involve testing your content using a variety of devices and assistive

technologies, as well as seeking feedback from users who may have unique accessibility needs. Be prepared to refine your interactive elements and animations based on this feedback, and always strive for continuous improvement.

10. Learning from examples and resources: One of the best ways to improve the accessibility of your animations and interactive elements is to learn from existing examples and resources. Many organizations and designers have created accessible animations and interactive elements that can serve as inspiration for your own work. Additionally, there are numerous resources available that can help you understand and apply accessibility best practices, such as the WCAG guidelines and various tutorials and articles on the subject.
11. Accommodating users with motion sensitivities: Users with vestibular disorders or motion sensitivities may experience discomfort or disorientation when viewing animations that include significant movement or parallax scrolling effects. To accommodate these users, consider providing alternative versions of your content without animations or with reduced motion. Alternatively, you can offer users the option to enable or disable motion effects according to their preferences.
12. Accessible progress indicators: When incorporating loading animations or progress indicators, it is important to ensure they are accessible. Provide alternative text or screen reader announcements to indicate the loading status or progress, so users relying on assistive technology can understand what is happening on the screen.

13. ARIA roles and attributes: When designing interactive elements, it is essential to use ARIA (Accessible Rich Internet Applications) roles and attributes. These help convey information about the element's function and state to screen reader users, improving the overall accessibility of your content. For example, ARIA roles can be used to indicate that an element is a button or a link, while ARIA attributes can convey information about the element's current state, such as whether it is expanded or collapsed.
14. Touch accessibility: With the increasing prevalence of touchscreen devices, it is crucial to ensure that your interactive elements are accessible to users who rely on touch input. Make sure that touch targets are large enough to be easily tapped, and that there is sufficient space between touch targets to minimize accidental taps. Additionally, test your interactive elements on a variety of touch devices to ensure they function correctly and are easy to use.
15. Accessible animations in instructional materials: When using animations in instructional materials or tutorials, ensure that they are accessible to all users by providing alternative formats, such as transcripts or static images, for those who cannot perceive or interact with the animations. Additionally, consider providing audio descriptions or captions for animations that include important auditory information.

As you strive to create a more inclusive and accessible digital experience, remember that considering the needs of all users is paramount.

9 / responsive and adaptive design for accessibility

mobile accessibility

THE RISE of smartphones and tablets has changed the way we access and interact with digital content. Today, many users rely on mobile devices as their primary means of accessing the internet. As a result, it is essential for designers and developers to consider mobile accessibility when creating digital experiences. In this section, we will explore the various aspects of mobile accessibility and discuss best practices for designing inclusive and user-friendly mobile experiences.

1. Touch-friendly interfaces: One of the most significant differences between traditional desktop and mobile experiences is the way users interact with content. On mobile devices, users typically rely on touch input instead of a keyboard and mouse. To create accessible mobile interfaces, ensure that touch targets are large enough to be easily tapped and that there is sufficient spacing between targets to avoid accidental taps. Additionally, consider implementing gesture-based

controls that are intuitive and easy to use for users with different motor abilities.

2. Screen size and orientation: Mobile devices come in various shapes and sizes, making it important to design flexible layouts that adapt to different screen dimensions and orientations. Responsive design techniques can help ensure that your content looks and functions well on a wide range of devices. Additionally, consider offering users the option to switch between portrait and landscape orientations to accommodate their preferences and specific accessibility needs.
3. Mobile font sizes and legibility: Text can be more challenging to read on smaller screens, so it's essential to choose legible fonts and appropriate font sizes for mobile devices. Stick to simple, sans-serif typefaces, and aim for a minimum font size of 16 pixels. Allow users to adjust the text size to meet their preferences and needs, and ensure that your layout adapts gracefully to different text sizes.
4. Mobile-specific navigation patterns: Navigation on mobile devices can be more challenging due to the limited screen real estate. To create accessible mobile navigation, consider using mobile-specific patterns like collapsible menus, tab bars, or bottom navigation bars. Ensure that these navigation elements are easy to locate, have clear labels, and are easy to interact with using touch input.
5. Accessible forms and controls: When designing forms for mobile devices, it's essential to make them accessible and easy to use. Choose form controls that are touch-friendly, such as dropdown menus, checkboxes, and radio buttons. Additionally, provide clear and concise labels for

each form field and ensure that error messages are informative and easy to understand.

6. Supporting mobile screen readers: Mobile devices also come with built-in screen readers, such as VoiceOver on iOS devices and TalkBack on Android devices. To ensure that your content is accessible to users who rely on these tools, follow best practices for using semantic markup, proper heading structure, and ARIA roles and attributes. Additionally, test your content with popular mobile screen readers to identify and fix any potential issues.
7. Accessible multimedia: As with desktop experiences, it's important to make multimedia content accessible on mobile devices. For video and audio content, provide captions, transcripts, and audio descriptions. For images, ensure that meaningful alternative text is provided. Be mindful of the size of multimedia files to avoid long loading times and excessive data usage, as this can be a barrier for users with limited data plans or slow internet connections.
8. Mobile performance and accessibility: Performance is a crucial aspect of mobile accessibility, as slow-loading content can be frustrating for all users, especially those with cognitive or attention-related disabilities. Optimize your content for fast loading times by compressing images, minifying code, and utilizing caching techniques. Additionally, consider implementing skeleton screens or other visual indicators to provide feedback on loading progress.
9. Mobile accessibility testing: Testing is a critical aspect of creating accessible mobile experiences. Use a combination of manual and automated testing tools to evaluate your content's accessibility

on various devices and operating systems. Test with real users, including those with disabilities, to gain valuable insights into how your content performs in real-world scenarios. Additionally, involve users with disabilities in the design process to ensure that their perspectives and needs are considered from the outset.

10. Mobile accessibility guidelines and standards: Just as with desktop experiences, mobile accessibility is governed by various guidelines and standards, such as the Web Content Accessibility Guidelines (WCAG) and the mobile-specific WAI-ARIA guidelines. Familiarize yourself with these guidelines and incorporate their recommendations into your mobile design and development processes.
11. Mobile operating system accessibility features: Both iOS and Android devices come with built-in accessibility features that can improve the user experience for people with disabilities. Examples include screen readers, magnification, and speech-to-text capabilities. As a designer or developer, it's important to be aware of these features and ensure that your content is compatible with them.
12. The role of progressive web apps (PWAs) in mobile accessibility: Progressive web apps (PWAs) offer a way to bridge the gap between mobile websites and native applications. By harnessing the power of modern web technologies, PWAs can provide a seamless, app-like experience that is accessible to a wide range of users and devices. When designing a PWA, be sure to follow best practices for both mobile and web accessibility to ensure that your app is inclusive and user-friendly.

Designing accessible mobile experiences is an essential part of creating inclusive digital content that caters to the needs and preferences of a diverse audience.

designing for different devices and screen sizes

Welcome to a world where technology is ever evolving, and the variety of devices and screen sizes that people use to access digital content is growing every day. As a designer or developer, it's crucial to create experiences that adapt seamlessly to different devices and screen sizes, ensuring that your content is accessible and enjoyable for all users. In this section, we will discuss some best practices and techniques for designing digital content that works well across a wide range of devices and screen sizes.

1. Embrace responsive design: Responsive design is a design approach that allows your content to adapt to different devices and screen sizes by using flexible layouts, images, and CSS media queries. This enables your content to automatically adjust to the user's device, ensuring that it looks great and functions optimally, whether they are viewing it on a smartphone, tablet, or desktop computer. Implementing responsive design is a must for modern websites and applications, as it helps to create a seamless user experience across various devices.
2. Design for mobile-first: With the growing number of people using mobile devices to access digital content, it's essential to prioritize designing for mobile users. Adopt a mobile-first approach, where you start by designing for smaller screens and then progressively enhance the design for larger screens.

This approach ensures that your content works well on the smallest devices and can take advantage of additional screen real estate as it becomes available.

3. Utilize fluid layouts and grids: Fluid layouts and grids provide a flexible structure for your content, allowing it to adjust to different screen sizes and orientations easily. By using relative units like percentages, your content will automatically resize and reflow based on the available screen space. This ensures that your design remains consistent and visually appealing, no matter what device it is being viewed on.
4. Consider touch interactions: As touch-screen devices become increasingly popular, it's crucial to consider how users will interact with your content using touch gestures. Ensure that interactive elements like buttons, links, and forms are large enough and spaced far enough apart to be easily tapped with a fingertip. Additionally, consider incorporating gesture-based navigation and interaction patterns, such as swiping or pinching, to create a more intuitive and engaging experience for touch-screen users.
5. Optimize images and multimedia: Images and multimedia content can greatly enhance the user experience, but they can also cause performance issues and slow load times if not properly optimized for different devices and screen sizes. Use responsive images and adaptive video techniques to serve appropriately sized media content based on the user's device and connection speed. This will ensure that your content loads quickly and looks great, regardless of the device being used.

6. Use CSS media queries: Media queries are a powerful tool for adapting your content to different devices and screen sizes. They allow you to apply specific CSS styles based on factors like device type, screen width, and screen orientation. Use media queries to fine-tune your design and ensure that it looks and functions optimally on various devices and screen sizes.
7. Test, test, test: It's essential to test your content on a variety of devices and screen sizes to ensure that it performs well and provides a consistent user experience. Use a combination of real devices, emulators, and browser-based testing tools to evaluate your design across multiple platforms and screen sizes. Additionally, seek feedback from real users to identify potential issues and areas for improvement.
8. Stay informed about new devices and trends: As technology continues to evolve, new devices with different screen sizes and capabilities will emerge. Stay informed about these trends and be prepared to adapt your design approach as needed to cater to the ever-changing landscape of digital devices.
9. Prioritize accessibility and inclusivity: When designing for different devices and screen sizes, always consider users with disabilities or limitations. Make sure that your content is accessible to everyone by following accessibility guidelines, such as the Web Content Accessibility Guidelines (WCAG), and including features like keyboard navigation, high-contrast color schemes, and alternative text for images.
10. Be mindful of performance: Performance is a crucial aspect of designing for different devices and screen sizes. Ensure that your content loads quickly

and runs smoothly on all devices by optimizing images, reducing the use of heavy scripts, and employing techniques like lazy loading and content delivery networks (CDNs).

11. Leverage design patterns: Familiar design patterns can help users navigate and interact with your content more easily, regardless of the device or screen size they are using. Consistently apply established design patterns, such as the hamburger menu for navigation or the card layout for displaying content, to create a seamless experience across different devices.
12. Use modular and component-based design: Breaking your design into smaller, reusable components can make it easier to adapt your content to different devices and screen sizes. By designing with a modular approach, you can ensure consistency and scalability, making it simpler to update and maintain your content across various platforms.
13. Iterate and refine: Designing for different devices and screen sizes is an ongoing process that requires continuous learning and adaptation. Regularly review your content's performance, gather feedback from users, and make improvements based on your findings. This iterative approach will help you create a more polished and effective experience for users across all devices and screen sizes.

By keeping these principles and techniques in mind, you can design digital content that is accessible, engaging, and enjoyable for users on any device and screen size.

touch and gesture accessibility

As we delve into the world of touch and gesture accessibility, it's essential to remember that designing for inclusivity means considering the wide range of ways users interact with digital content. Touchscreens and gesture-based interactions are becoming increasingly popular in our daily lives, from smartphones and tablets to interactive kiosks and wearables. As a result, it's crucial to ensure that these interactions are accessible to everyone, including users with different abilities and preferences.

1. Understanding the importance of touch and gesture accessibility: When we talk about touch and gesture accessibility, we're referring to the ease with which users can navigate and interact with digital content using touchscreens and gestures. For users with motor impairments, visual impairments, or cognitive disabilities, touch and gesture interactions can present unique challenges. By addressing these challenges, we can create more inclusive digital experiences for all users.
2. Guidelines for touch target sizes: One of the most critical aspects of touch accessibility is ensuring that interactive elements, such as buttons, links, and form controls, are large enough to be easily tapped by users. The Web Content Accessibility Guidelines (WCAG) recommend a minimum touch target size of 44x44 pixels for interactive elements. By adhering to this guideline, you can make it easier for users with motor impairments or limited dexterity to interact with your content.
3. Providing ample spacing between touch targets: In addition to the size of touch targets, it's important to consider the spacing between them. Users with

motor impairments may have difficulty accurately tapping small, closely spaced targets. Ensure there is enough space between touch targets to reduce the likelihood of accidental taps and make it easier for users to interact with your content.

4. Supporting a variety of gestures: Touchscreens and gesture-based interactions often rely on a variety of gestures, such as swiping, pinching, and tapping. To make your content accessible to users with different abilities, it's essential to support multiple gestures and provide alternative methods for performing the same action. For example, you might allow users to swipe through a photo gallery or tap on arrow buttons to navigate between images.
5. Offering alternatives to gesture-based interactions: Some users may have difficulty performing certain gestures due to motor impairments or other limitations. In these cases, it's crucial to provide alternative methods for interacting with your content. This might include offering keyboard shortcuts, on-screen controls, or voice commands as alternative ways to perform common actions.
6. Prioritizing simplicity and clarity in gesture-based interactions: When designing touch and gesture interactions, strive for simplicity and clarity. Complex gestures or multi-step interactions can be challenging for users with cognitive disabilities or those who are new to touch-based interfaces. By keeping gestures simple and easy to understand, you can create more accessible and user-friendly experiences.
7. Providing clear instructions and feedback: Clear instructions and feedback are essential for ensuring that users understand how to interact with your

content using touch and gestures. Make sure to provide concise, easy-to-understand instructions for performing gestures, and offer immediate feedback to users, such as visual or auditory cues, when they successfully complete a gesture.

8. Testing and refining touch and gesture interactions: As with any aspect of accessibility, it's important to test and refine your touch and gesture interactions to ensure they are accessible and usable for all users. Gather feedback from users with different abilities, and use this feedback to make improvements and optimize your touch and gesture interactions.
9. Be mindful of touch and gesture interactions for users with visual impairments: Users with visual impairments rely on screen readers or other assistive technologies to interact with digital content. When designing touch and gesture interactions, consider how these users will navigate your content. Ensure that your touch targets are labeled correctly so screen readers can announce them, and provide alternative ways to navigate your content, such as keyboard shortcuts or voice commands.
10. Considering the impact of device orientation on touch and gesture accessibility: As users interact with digital content on different devices and screen sizes, it's essential to consider how device orientation might impact touch and gesture accessibility. For example, when a user switches from portrait to landscape mode on a smartphone, touch targets may become smaller or more difficult to reach. Be sure to test your content in different orientations and address any potential issues that may arise.

11. Addressing the needs of users with hearing impairments: While touch and gesture interactions are primarily focused on users with motor and visual impairments, it's important to consider the needs of users with hearing impairments as well. For example, if your content includes auditory feedback or cues, ensure that there are also visual alternatives available, such as on-screen text or icons.
12. Designing for users with cognitive impairments: When designing touch and gesture interactions, be mindful of users with cognitive impairments who may have difficulty understanding complex interactions or remembering multi-step gestures. Prioritize simplicity and clarity, and provide clear instructions and feedback to support these users.
13. Continuous learning and staying up to date with accessibility best practices: As technology and accessibility standards continue to evolve, it's important to stay informed about the latest best practices and guidelines for touch and gesture accessibility. Regularly review accessibility resources, attend webinars or conferences, and engage with the accessibility community to ensure your content remains accessible and inclusive for all users.

In this ever-evolving world of touch and gesture-based technology, we must make accessibility a priority.

part three
evaluating and implementing accessibility

10 / accessibility testing

automated testing tools

IN OUR JOURNEY TO create accessible digital content, one of the key aspects is ensuring that our work is in line with accessibility standards and best practices. While manual testing is essential, it can be time-consuming, and there's always a possibility of human error. This is where automated testing tools come into play, helping us identify accessibility issues and work towards a more inclusive digital experience. In this section, we'll dive into the world of automated testing tools, exploring their benefits and limitations, and how to choose the right tool for your needs.

Automated testing tools are software applications that help you evaluate the accessibility of your digital content by checking it against established guidelines, such as the Web Content Accessibility Guidelines (WCAG). These tools can quickly and efficiently scan your website or application, identify potential accessibility issues, and provide suggestions for remediation. They are particularly useful for catching common issues like missing alternative text for images, incorrect markup, and color contrast problems.

Advantages of using automated testing tools include:

1. Speed and efficiency: Automated testing tools can quickly scan a large volume of content, saving you time and effort compared to manual testing.
2. Consistency: These tools follow a consistent set of rules, reducing the risk of human error and ensuring a uniform evaluation of your content.
3. Easy integration: Many automated testing tools can be integrated into your development process, allowing you to identify and address accessibility issues early on.
4. Reporting: Automated testing tools typically generate detailed reports that help you track progress, prioritize issues, and maintain an audit trail for compliance purposes.

However, automated testing tools also have their limitations:

1. Inability to evaluate all accessibility issues: While these tools can detect many common issues, they can't assess every aspect of accessibility, such as whether content makes sense when read by a screen reader. Manual testing is still necessary for a complete evaluation.
2. False positives and negatives: Automated testing tools may sometimes flag issues that aren't genuine problems or miss actual issues. Human judgment is required to validate the findings.
3. Limited context: These tools can't always understand the context of your content, which may lead to incorrect evaluations or recommendations.

To make the most of automated testing tools, consider the following tips:

1. Choose the right tool: There are numerous automated testing tools available, each with its strengths and weaknesses. Some tools focus on specific aspects of accessibility, while others provide a more comprehensive evaluation. Consider your needs, budget, and the level of integration you require before selecting a tool.
2. Combine automated testing with manual testing: Automated testing tools are a valuable resource, but they can't replace the insights gained through manual testing. Ensure you allocate time and resources for both approaches to achieve a comprehensive evaluation of your digital content.
3. Validate the results: As mentioned earlier, automated testing tools may generate false positives or negatives. It's essential to review the results, validate the issues identified, and prioritize the most critical problems to address.
4. Integrate accessibility testing into your development process: To create accessible content from the outset, incorporate automated testing tools into your development workflow. This will help you identify and address accessibility issues early on, saving time and resources in the long run.
5. Keep learning and staying informed: Accessibility standards and best practices are constantly evolving. Stay up-to-date with the latest developments in the field and adjust your testing strategies accordingly.

As you continue to explore the world of automated testing tools, you might wonder which specific tools are worth considering. While there are numerous options available, some popular and widely-used automated testing tools include:

1. Axe: Developed by Deque Systems, Axe is an open-source accessibility testing tool that can be used as a browser extension or integrated into your development process. It's known for its accuracy, speed, and ability to minimize false positives.
2. WAVE: WebAIM's WAVE is a browser extension and online service that evaluates the accessibility of web pages. WAVE provides a visual representation of potential issues, making it easy to identify and understand the problems.
3. Lighthouse: Created by Google, Lighthouse is an open-source tool that audits the performance, accessibility, and other aspects of web pages. It can be run in Chrome DevTools, as a browser extension, or as a command-line tool.
4. Tenon.io: Tenon.io is a web-based accessibility testing tool that offers a comprehensive evaluation of your content, along with detailed reports and recommendations. It also provides integration with various content management systems, task management tools, and development workflows.
5. Siteimprove: Siteimprove is a comprehensive digital optimization platform that includes accessibility testing, SEO, analytics, and more. It offers robust reporting and prioritizes accessibility issues based on their impact.

When evaluating these tools, remember that no single tool can catch every accessibility issue. It's a good idea to use multiple tools or combine them with manual testing to gain a more comprehensive understanding of your content's accessibility.

To maximize the benefits of automated testing tools, consider adopting the following best practices:

1. Train your team: Ensure that your team members, including developers, designers, and content creators, are familiar with accessibility principles and the tools you've chosen. This will help them understand and act upon the findings generated by the automated testing tools.
2. Develop a testing plan: Creating a structured testing plan can help you track progress and ensure that you're addressing all aspects of accessibility. Outline the tools and techniques you'll use, as well as the testing schedule and the roles and responsibilities of team members.
3. Encourage collaboration: Foster a collaborative environment where team members can share their knowledge and experiences with accessibility testing. This can lead to improved problem-solving and the discovery of new testing techniques.
4. Track progress and measure success: Use the reporting features of your chosen automated testing tools to monitor progress, identify trends, and measure the success of your accessibility efforts. Regularly review this data and adjust your strategy as needed.
5. Continuously iterate and improve: Accessibility is not a one-time effort but an ongoing process. Continuously review and update your content, incorporating user feedback and staying informed about the latest developments in accessibility standards and best practices.

Automated testing tools can be a valuable addition to your accessibility toolkit, helping you identify and address issues more efficiently.

manual testing techniques

Let's talk about manual testing techniques. While automated testing tools can certainly help you identify a variety of accessibility issues, manual testing remains an essential component of any comprehensive accessibility strategy. By complementing automated testing with manual techniques, you can ensure that your digital content is accessible to users with diverse needs and preferences.

In this section, we'll explore a variety of manual testing techniques that can help you assess and improve the accessibility of your content. So, grab your favorite beverage, and let's dive in!

1. Keyboard-only navigation: One of the simplest yet most effective manual testing techniques is navigating your website or application using only the keyboard. This simulates the experience of users who cannot use a mouse or other pointing devices. To perform this test, use the Tab key to navigate through interactive elements and verify that all controls can be accessed and operated. Also, ensure that the focus order is logical and predictable, and that a clear focus indicator is visible.
2. Screen reader testing: Many users with visual impairments rely on screen readers to access digital content. To perform screen reader testing, you can use popular screen readers like JAWS (Job Access With Speech), NVDA (NonVisual Desktop Access), or VoiceOver (Apple's built-in screen reader). As

you navigate your content with a screen reader, verify that all elements are announced correctly, and that the reading order is logical and meaningful.

3. Zoom and magnification testing: Some users may need to enlarge content to make it more legible. To test for this, zoom in on your content using the browser's built-in zoom controls or a screen magnifier like Windows Magnifier or macOS Zoom. Check that the layout and functionality remain intact and that all content remains readable and usable.
4. Color contrast and color-blindness testing: Ensure that your content has sufficient color contrast and can be easily understood by users with various types of color vision deficiencies. To do this, you can use color contrast analyzers like the WebAIM Color Contrast Checker, and simulate different types of color blindness using browser extensions like NoCoffee or Sim Daltonism.
5. Voice control testing: Some users may rely on voice control to interact with your content. You can test your website or application with voice control software like Dragon NaturallySpeaking (for Windows) or the built-in macOS Voice Control feature. Verify that all interactive elements can be successfully activated and manipulated using voice commands.
6. Cognitive accessibility testing: Cognitive accessibility involves making your content comprehensible and usable for users with cognitive or learning disabilities. This might involve testing the readability of your text using tools like the Hemingway Editor or the Flesch-Kincaid

Readability Test, and assessing the clarity and simplicity of your content and user interface.

7. Usability testing with diverse users: Finally, one of the most valuable manual testing techniques involves conducting usability tests with users who have different disabilities or accessibility needs. By observing how these users interact with your content, you can identify potential barriers and gain valuable insights into how to make your content more accessible and inclusive.

As you embark on your journey to create more accessible content, keep in mind that

As you work with manual testing techniques, you might find some additional resources helpful. Many organizations and experts in the field of digital accessibility have compiled best practices, guidelines, and checklists that you can use to support your manual testing efforts. Some of these resources include:

1. Web Content Accessibility Guidelines (WCAG): Developed by the World Wide Web Consortium (W3C), the WCAG is a comprehensive set of guidelines and recommendations that provide a solid foundation for ensuring digital accessibility. Reviewing and understanding these guidelines can help inform your manual testing efforts.
2. WebAIM (Web Accessibility In Mind): WebAIM is a reputable organization that provides a wealth of resources, articles, and tools related to digital accessibility. Their website is a treasure trove of information and guidance that can support your manual testing process.
3. A11Y Project: The A11Y Project is a community-driven effort to provide practical accessibility

resources and guidance. They offer a variety of checklists, articles, and tools that can help you implement and assess the accessibility of your content.
4. Local and online accessibility communities: Connecting with others who share your interest in accessibility can be invaluable in terms of learning, sharing experiences, and seeking advice. Look for local meetups, conferences, or online forums where you can engage with accessibility enthusiasts and experts.

By utilizing these resources and staying informed about the latest developments in the field of digital accessibility, you can continually refine your manual testing techniques and ensure that your content remains accessible and inclusive for all users.

Manual testing techniques play a vital role in assessing and improving the accessibility of your digital content.

inclusive user testing

Let's dive into the exciting world of inclusive user testing! In this section, we'll discuss the importance of involving users with diverse abilities and backgrounds in the testing process, and how you can make your user testing more inclusive. By the end, you'll be equipped with the knowledge and tools to make your digital experiences more accessible and enjoyable for everyone.

Why is inclusive user testing important? As you may already know, designing and developing accessible digital content is essential to ensure that your products and services are usable by people with diverse abilities, including those with disabilities. But just as important is the process of testing your content to make sure it meets the needs of all users.

Inclusive user testing involves engaging people with different abilities, backgrounds, and experiences in the evaluation process. This helps ensure that your digital content doesn't just meet technical accessibility standards, but also works well in real-world scenarios for people with a wide range of abilities and preferences. Including diverse perspectives in your testing process can uncover issues that you might have missed otherwise, leading to a more accessible and user-friendly end product.

Now that we understand the importance of inclusive user testing, let's explore some strategies for incorporating it into your testing process.

1. Recruit diverse participants: Actively seek out participants who represent a wide range of abilities, backgrounds, and experiences. This might include people with disabilities, older adults, individuals who are not native speakers of your content's language, and those with different levels of technical expertise.
2. Be mindful of accessibility during the testing process: Ensure that your testing environment, materials, and tools are accessible for all participants. This might involve providing screen readers or other assistive technology, offering alternate formats for written materials, or ensuring that your testing facility is wheelchair accessible.
3. Adapt testing tasks to accommodate different abilities: Modify tasks or scenarios to accommodate the unique needs and preferences of each participant. For example, you might ask a participant who uses a screen reader to explore your website and provide feedback on their experience, rather than asking them to perform a

specific task that may not be relevant to their typical usage.

4. Encourage open communication: Create a comfortable environment in which participants feel free to share their thoughts, feelings, and concerns. This can help you gain valuable insights into their experiences and uncover potential accessibility issues.
5. Analyze and apply feedback: Carefully review the feedback gathered during user testing and use it to inform your design and development decisions. Be open to making changes based on the insights you gain from diverse users, even if it means rethinking some of your initial assumptions.
6. Continuously iterate and improve: Inclusive user testing isn't a one-time event. As you make changes to your digital content, continue to involve diverse users in the testing process to ensure that your improvements are effective and beneficial for everyone.
7. Collaborate with accessibility experts: While it's important to involve diverse users in your testing process, it's also beneficial to collaborate with accessibility professionals who can provide guidance and expertise. They can help you identify potential issues, suggest improvements, and ensure that your content meets accessibility standards and guidelines.
8. Use a mix of quantitative and qualitative methods: While it's essential to gather qualitative feedback from users during inclusive user testing, don't overlook the value of quantitative data as well. Combining both types of data can help you identify trends, prioritize improvements, and measure the impact of your accessibility efforts.

9. Develop empathy and understanding: As you engage with diverse users during the testing process, strive to develop a deeper empathy and understanding of their needs, preferences, and challenges. This can help you become a more compassionate and effective advocate for accessibility within your organization.
10. Share your findings and advocate for change: After conducting inclusive user testing, be sure to share your findings with your team, stakeholders, and other relevant parties. Use your findings to advocate for changes and improvements that will benefit all users, and to raise awareness about the importance of accessibility and inclusion.
11. Keep up-to-date with accessibility trends and best practices: The world of digital accessibility is constantly evolving, and it's crucial to stay informed about the latest trends, guidelines, and best practices. Regularly attending webinars, conferences, and workshops, as well as following accessibility-focused blogs and social media accounts, can help you stay current and continue to improve your skills.
12. Create a culture of accessibility: To truly make a difference and ensure that your digital content is accessible to everyone; it's important to foster a culture of accessibility within your organization. Encourage your team members to prioritize accessibility, provide training and resources to help them develop their skills, and celebrate your successes along the way.

By following these tips and best practices, you can create a more robust and effective inclusive user testing process. Remember that the goal is to make your digital content accessible and enjoyable for everyone, and that requires ongoing learning, collaboration, and improvement.

As we wrap up this section on inclusive user testing, we hope that you feel inspired and empowered to make a positive impact in the world of digital accessibility. With the knowledge and tools you've gained, you're well on your way to creating more inclusive and accessible experiences that truly benefit all users. Keep learning, keep iterating, and keep advocating for a more accessible digital world for everyone.

11 / integrating accessibility into the design process

accessibility audits and checklists

ACCESSIBILITY AUDITS and checklists are essential components of creating a more accessible digital experience. An audit is a thorough assessment of your website or application to determine how well it complies with accessibility guidelines and standards. A checklist, on the other hand, is a practical tool that can help you track your progress, stay organized, and ensure that you're addressing every aspect of accessibility. In this section, we'll delve into the process of conducting accessibility audits and the benefits of using checklists to streamline your efforts.

Before we dive into the details of accessibility audits, it's important to understand the value of conducting these assessments. The primary goal of an audit is to identify any barriers or issues that could prevent users with disabilities from accessing or using your digital content. By uncovering these issues, you can then make the necessary improvements to ensure that your website or application is more inclusive and accessible to all users.

To conduct a comprehensive accessibility audit, follow these steps:

1. Review accessibility guidelines and standards: Familiarize yourself with the most widely recognized accessibility guidelines, such as the Web Content Accessibility Guidelines (WCAG), which outline the best practices for making digital content more accessible to users with disabilities.
2. Define the scope of your audit: Determine which parts of your website or application will be included in the audit. This might include specific pages, sections, or features, depending on the size and complexity of your digital content.
3. Create an audit plan: Develop a clear plan outlining the steps you'll take during the audit process, including the tools and methods you'll use to assess your digital content.
4. Conduct automated testing: Use automated testing tools to quickly identify accessibility issues, such as missing alt text, incorrect heading structures, or insufficient color contrast.
5. Perform manual testing: While automated tools can be incredibly helpful, they won't catch every accessibility issue. Manual testing, which involves navigating and interacting with your digital content using various assistive technologies (such as screen readers, keyboard navigation, and voice control), is crucial for identifying issues that may not be detected by automated testing.
6. Involve users with disabilities: Engaging users with disabilities in the audit process can provide valuable insights into their unique experiences and help you uncover issues that you may not have considered.
7. Document your findings: As you conduct your audit, keep detailed notes about any issues you

discover, as well as any potential solutions or improvements.

8. Prioritize and implement improvements: Once your audit is complete, prioritize the issues you've identified and create a plan for addressing them. Implement the necessary changes and monitor your progress to ensure that your digital content becomes more accessible over time.

Now, let's explore the role of checklists in the accessibility audit process. A checklist is a valuable tool that can help you stay organized, track your progress, and ensure that you're addressing every aspect of accessibility. Here are some tips for creating and using accessibility checklists:

1. Start with a comprehensive template: There are many accessibility checklists available online, which can serve as a starting point for your own customized checklist. Look for checklists that are based on established guidelines, such as the WCAG, and adapt them to suit your specific needs.
2. Organize your checklist by categories: Break down your checklist into categories, such as navigation, content structure, images, and forms, to make it easier to manage and navigate.
3. Use clear and concise language: Write your checklist items in a clear and straightforward manner to ensure that they're easy to understand and follow.
4. Include specific examples: Provide examples and explanations for each item on your checklist to help clarify the requirements and expectations.
5. Make your checklist actionable: For each item on your checklist, include a clear action or task that can be completed to address the issue.

6. Update your checklist regularly: As accessibility guidelines and best practices evolve over time, it's important to keep your checklist up to date. Regularly review and update your checklist to ensure that it reflects the latest accessibility standards and recommendations.
7. Use your checklist as a reference during audits: Refer to your checklist throughout the audit process to help guide your assessment and ensure that you're considering every aspect of accessibility.
8. Track your progress: As you complete each item on your checklist, mark it as done or note any outstanding issues that need to be addressed. This will help you monitor your progress and stay on track with your accessibility goals.
9. Share your checklist with your team: Encourage collaboration and shared responsibility for accessibility by making your checklist available to your entire team. This can help foster a culture of accessibility within your organization and ensure that everyone is on the same page.
10. Learn from your experiences: As you conduct audits and work through your checklist, take note of any recurring issues or areas where you're consistently encountering challenges. Use this information to refine your checklist and improve your accessibility efforts moving forward.

Accessibility audits and checklists are vital tools for identifying and addressing barriers that could prevent users with disabilities from accessing or using your digital content. By conducting thorough audits and utilizing well-organized checklists, you can ensure that your website or application is more inclusive, accessible, and user-friendly for everyone.

collaboration between designers, developers, and content creators

Creating a truly accessible and inclusive digital experience requires a collaborative effort from every member of the team, including designers, developers, and content creators. In this section, we'll explore how effective collaboration between these groups can lead to better accessibility outcomes and a more satisfying user experience for everyone.

1. Establish a shared understanding of accessibility goals: Start by ensuring that all team members have a clear understanding of the accessibility goals for the project. This includes being familiar with accessibility guidelines, such as the Web Content Accessibility Guidelines (WCAG), and understanding the needs of users with various disabilities. A shared understanding of accessibility goals will help everyone work together more effectively and make informed decisions throughout the project.
2. Foster a culture of accessibility: Encourage a culture of accessibility within your team by emphasizing its importance and providing opportunities for education and training. Make accessibility a priority from the outset of every project and regularly discuss its progress during team meetings. This will help to create a shared sense of responsibility and commitment to accessibility among all team members.
3. Collaborative planning and design: Involve designers, developers, and content creators in the planning and design process from the beginning. This can help identify potential accessibility issues early on and ensure that everyone is working

towards a common goal. When designers and developers understand each other's roles and constraints, they can work together to create solutions that are both visually appealing and technically feasible.

4. Clear communication channels: Establish clear communication channels among team members to share ideas, feedback, and concerns related to accessibility. This can include regular team meetings, email threads, or project management tools. Encourage open dialogue and active listening, and provide a safe space for team members to voice their opinions and concerns.
5. Define roles and responsibilities: Clearly outline the roles and responsibilities of each team member with regard to accessibility. This will help to prevent confusion and ensure that accessibility remains a priority throughout the project. For example, designers may be responsible for creating accessible visual elements, developers for implementing accessible code, and content creators for producing accessible content.
6. Use accessible design and development tools: Make sure that the tools used by the team, such as design software or content management systems, are accessible and support the creation of accessible content. This will enable team members to work together more efficiently and ensure that accessibility is embedded into the project from the start.
7. Continuous collaboration and feedback: Encourage team members to collaborate and provide feedback throughout the project, not just during the initial planning and design stages. This can help to identify and address accessibility

issues as they arise and ensure that everyone remains committed to creating an accessible end product.

8. Test and iterate: Regularly test your website or application for accessibility issues throughout the development process, using both automated testing tools and manual testing techniques. This will help to identify and address issues early on, making it easier for the team to work together to create an accessible final product.
9. Include users with disabilities in the design and development process: One of the most effective ways to ensure that your website or application is accessible is to involve users with disabilities in the design and development process. This can include user testing, focus groups, or interviews. By involving users with disabilities, you can gain valuable insights into their needs and preferences, which can help to inform your design and development decisions.
10. Celebrate successes and learn from challenges: As you work together to create an accessible digital experience, take the time to celebrate your successes and acknowledge the hard work of your team members. At the same time, be open to learning from any challenges or setbacks that you encounter along the way. This will help to foster a positive and supportive team environment, in which everyone feels motivated to continue working towards better accessibility outcomes.
11. Document and share best practices: As your team develops expertise in accessible design and development, document your best practices and share them within your organization. This can help to spread awareness of accessibility and provide a

valuable resource for other teams working on similar projects.

12. Leverage the expertise of accessibility specialists: When possible, involve accessibility specialists in your project to provide guidance and recommendations. These experts can offer valuable insights and help to ensure that your team is adhering to best practices in accessibility.
13. Create a feedback loop with users: Establish a feedback loop with users, including those with disabilities, to gather input on your website or application's accessibility. This feedback can help you identify areas for improvement and prioritize future updates. Be open to receiving constructive criticism and use it as an opportunity to learn and grow.
14. Stay informed about accessibility trends and advancements: As technology evolves, so do accessibility standards and best practices. Stay informed about the latest trends and advancements in the field of digital accessibility by attending conferences, participating in webinars, and following industry thought leaders. This will help your team to stay up-to-date with the latest techniques and tools that can improve your website or application's accessibility.
15. Continuously refine your processes: As you learn from your successes and challenges, take the time to refine your processes and improve your team's approach to accessibility. This might involve updating your internal guidelines, adjusting your project management approach, or adopting new tools and technologies.

Collaboration between designers, developers, and content

creators is essential for creating truly accessible digital experiences.

iterative design for continuous improvement

Embracing iterative design is essential for creating accessible and user-friendly digital experiences. In this section, we'll dive deep into the world of iterative design and explore its importance in the context of accessibility. We'll discuss how this design approach can lead to continuous improvement in your digital products and how your team can adopt it as a core design principle.

The concept of iterative design revolves around making incremental improvements to a product based on user feedback and ongoing testing. It's a dynamic process that involves continuous learning, adaptation, and refinement. This approach can be particularly valuable when it comes to ensuring accessibility, as it allows teams to identify and address issues more effectively and efficiently.

To effectively implement iterative design in your projects, consider the following steps:

1. Set the stage for iterative design: Start by creating an environment where iterative design is encouraged and supported. This may involve fostering a culture of experimentation and learning within your team, as well as setting up processes and tools to facilitate iterative design.
2. Begin with research: Before diving into design and development, conduct thorough research on your target audience, including their needs, preferences, and any potential accessibility challenges. This will help you create a solid foundation for your design process and ensure

that you're addressing the most critical issues from the outset.

3. Develop a prototype: Create a rough prototype of your design, focusing on the most essential elements and functionality. This prototype will serve as a starting point for your iterative design process and help you to identify areas where improvements can be made.
4. Test early and often: Begin testing your prototype as soon as possible, seeking feedback from users, including those with disabilities. This early testing will help you identify potential issues and make adjustments before investing significant time and resources into development.
5. Analyze feedback and refine: Analyze the feedback you receive from testing, looking for patterns and trends that can inform your design decisions. Use this information to refine your prototype, addressing any issues or concerns that have been identified.
6. Repeat the process: Continue to iterate on your design, testing and refining as you go. With each iteration, your product will become more accessible, user-friendly, and polished.
7. Keep track of your progress: Document your iterative design process, including any changes you make, feedback received, and lessons learned. This documentation can be valuable for future projects and help your team to continuously improve its approach to accessibility.
8. Stay flexible and adaptable: Recognize that iterative design is an ongoing process that requires flexibility and adaptability. Be open to changing course or making significant adjustments to your design as you learn more about your users and their needs.

9. Encourage collaboration: Iterative design is most effective when it's a collaborative effort that involves input from designers, developers, content creators, and other stakeholders. Foster a collaborative environment where everyone feels comfortable sharing their ideas, feedback, and concerns.
10. Celebrate your successes: Take the time to acknowledge and celebrate the improvements you've made through your iterative design process. This can help to build momentum and motivate your team to continue striving for excellence in accessibility.

Iterative design is a powerful approach that can help you create more accessible and user-friendly digital products. By embracing this process and continuously refining your design based on user feedback and testing, you can make significant strides in improving the accessibility of your website or application.

12 / accessibility laws and compliance

overview of accessibility laws and regulations

UNDERSTANDING the landscape of accessibility laws and regulations is crucial for ensuring your digital products comply with the necessary requirements. In this section, we'll provide an overview of some of the most significant accessibility laws and regulations worldwide, including the United States, the European Union, Canada, and Australia. By familiarizing yourself with these requirements, you can be better equipped to create inclusive and accessible digital experiences for all users.

United States: Section 508 and the Americans with Disabilities Act (ADA)

In the United States, two key pieces of legislation govern accessibility: Section 508 and the Americans with Disabilities Act (ADA). Section 508 is part of the Rehabilitation Act of 1973, which requires federal agencies to ensure their electronic and information technology is accessible to people with disabilities. This includes websites, software, hardware, and electronic documents.

The ADA, enacted in 1990, is a comprehensive civil rights

law that prohibits discrimination against individuals with disabilities. Title II of the ADA applies to state and local government entities, while Title III covers public accommodations, which include most businesses and non-profit organizations. Although the ADA does not explicitly mention websites or digital products, court rulings and guidance from the Department of Justice have made it clear that digital accessibility falls under the scope of the ADA.

European Union: Web Accessibility Directive and European Accessibility Act

In the European Union (EU), the Web Accessibility Directive and the European Accessibility Act (EAA) are key pieces of legislation governing accessibility. The Web Accessibility Directive, which came into force in 2016, requires all public sector websites and mobile applications to be accessible, following the Web Content Accessibility Guidelines (WCAG) 2.1 Level AA.

The EAA, adopted in 2019, is a broader piece of legislation that covers various aspects of accessibility, including digital products and services. The EAA applies to both public and private sector organizations and sets accessibility requirements for computers, operating systems, smartphones, tablets, digital services, e-commerce, e-books, and more.

Canada: Accessible Canada Act and provincial legislation

In Canada, the Accessible Canada Act (ACA) is the federal law governing accessibility. Enacted in 2019, the ACA aims to achieve a barrier-free Canada by 2040. It applies to federally regulated organizations and sets accessibility standards for areas such as employment, built environments, information and communication technologies, procurement, and transportation.

In addition to the ACA, several provinces in Canada have their own accessibility legislation. For example, Ontario has the Accessibility for Ontarians with Disabilities Act (AODA), which requires organizations to meet specific accessibility standards, including those for websites and web content.

Australia: Disability Discrimination Act

In Australia, the Disability Discrimination Act (DDA) is the primary legislation governing accessibility. Enacted in 1992, the DDA makes it unlawful to discriminate against individuals with disabilities in various areas, including access to goods, services, and facilities. Although the DDA does not explicitly mention websites or digital products, the Australian Human Rights Commission has provided guidance that indicates digital accessibility falls under the scope of the DDA.

To ensure compliance with these laws and regulations, it's essential to familiarize yourself with the specific accessibility standards they reference, such as the WCAG. By adhering to these standards, you can create digital products that are more inclusive and accessible to all users, while also reducing the risk of legal action.

Beyond legal compliance, there are many reasons to prioritize accessibility in your digital products. When you make your digital content accessible, you're not only helping individuals with disabilities; you're also improving usability for all users. For example, accessible design often leads to better SEO, improved navigation, and easier interaction on different devices.

When working on accessibility initiatives, it's essential to engage various stakeholders, including designers, developers, content creators, and end-users. By fostering a culture of collaboration and open communication, you can ensure that accessibility is considered throughout the entire design and development process.

In some cases, organizations may need to consult with experts or seek out additional resources to better understand the complexities of accessibility laws and regulations. Professional organizations, such as the International Association of Accessibility Professionals (IAAP), can offer valuable guidance and resources to help you navigate the world of accessibility compliance.

Finally, keep in mind that accessibility is an ongoing process. As technology evolves, so too must our understanding of accessibility best practices. Regularly reviewing and updating your digital products to meet new accessibility standards will ensure that you continue to provide inclusive experiences for all users.

meeting legal requirements

Meeting legal requirements for digital accessibility is an essential part of creating inclusive products and services. It's important to recognize that the process of achieving compliance goes beyond simply checking off boxes on a list. Meeting legal requirements involves understanding the needs of people with disabilities, implementing accessibility best practices, and continually refining your digital products to provide the best possible user experience.

Before diving into the specifics, let's first understand why it's crucial to meet legal requirements for accessibility. For one, you'll be protecting your organization from potential legal action. Numerous lawsuits have been filed against businesses for failing to provide accessible digital experiences. By ensuring that your products meet legal requirements, you'll be minimizing the risk of facing costly litigation.

Additionally, meeting legal requirements can lead to improved customer satisfaction and brand reputation. When your digital products are accessible to a broader audience, you're demonstrating that your organization values inclusivity and is committed to providing equal access to all users.

Now that we've discussed the importance of meeting legal requirements, let's explore some practical tips for achieving compliance:

1. Familiarize yourself with relevant laws and regulations: The first step is to understand the accessibility laws and regulations that apply to your organization. These can vary depending on your location and industry. Key legislation to be aware of includes the Americans with Disabilities Act (ADA) in the United States, the European Union's Web Accessibility Directive, and the Accessibility for Ontarians with Disabilities Act (AODA) in Canada. There are many other regional and industry-specific regulations, so be sure to research the ones that are relevant to your organization.
2. Adhere to established accessibility standards: The World Wide Web Consortium (W3C) has developed the Web Content Accessibility Guidelines (WCAG), which serve as the international standard for digital accessibility. These guidelines provide a comprehensive framework to help you create digital products that are accessible to all users. Make sure your organization is familiar with WCAG and follows the guidelines in your design and development processes.
3. Implement accessibility from the start: One of the most effective ways to meet legal requirements is to integrate accessibility from the beginning of your design and development processes. This means considering accessibility during the ideation, wireframing, and prototyping phases, and continuing to prioritize it throughout development and testing. By incorporating accessibility from the start, you'll be able to identify and address potential issues early on, reducing the need for costly and time-consuming fixes later.

4. Train your team: Ensuring that your team is knowledgeable about accessibility best practices is crucial for meeting legal requirements. Provide training and resources to your designers, developers, and content creators to help them understand the importance of accessibility and how to implement it effectively. Encourage a culture of continuous learning, and stay up to date on emerging trends and best practices in accessibility.
5. Conduct regular audits: Regularly evaluate your digital products for accessibility compliance using a combination of automated testing tools, manual testing techniques, and user testing with individuals with disabilities. This will help you identify areas where your products may not meet legal requirements, allowing you to address these issues proactively.
6. Document your accessibility efforts: Keeping a record of your organization's accessibility initiatives, policies, and procedures can help demonstrate your commitment to accessibility and provide evidence of compliance in the event of legal action. Be transparent about your accessibility efforts, and share your progress with stakeholders, customers, and the public.
7. Seek expert guidance: If you're unsure about how to meet legal requirements, consider consulting with accessibility experts who can provide guidance and support. They can help you identify potential issues, suggest appropriate solutions, and ensure that your digital products are fully compliant with applicable laws and regulations.

To summarize, here are the key points to keep in mind

when working towards meeting legal requirements for digital accessibility:

1. Understand the accessibility laws and regulations that apply to your organization and industry.
2. Follow established accessibility standards, such as the WCAG.
3. Incorporate accessibility best practices from the beginning of your design and development processes.
4. Train your team members and foster a culture of continuous learning around accessibility.
5. Conduct regular audits to evaluate and improve the accessibility of your digital products.
6. Document your accessibility efforts and be transparent about your progress.
7. Seek expert guidance and collaborate with others to achieve accessibility goals.

By following these guidelines and maintaining a commitment to continuous improvement, your organization will be well-equipped to meet legal requirements and create digital products that are accessible to all users.

best practices for documentation and reporting

Throughout our journey in this book, we've explored various aspects of digital accessibility. We've learned about the importance of creating accessible products and services, and we've delved into the details of design, development, and testing to ensure accessibility. As we draw closer to the end of our exploration, let's turn our attention to an equally important aspect of accessibility: documentation and reporting.

Proper documentation and reporting are essential to

demonstrate your organization's commitment to digital accessibility. They can help you keep track of your progress, identify areas for improvement, and serve as valuable evidence of compliance with accessibility laws and regulations. In this section, we'll explore best practices for documentation and reporting that will help your organization maintain and improve its accessibility efforts.

- Create an accessibility policy and statement

An accessibility policy is a formal document that outlines your organization's commitment to digital accessibility. It should provide clear guidelines on how your organization will work to ensure that its products and services are accessible to all users, including those with disabilities. Additionally, an accessibility statement is a public-facing document that communicates your commitment to accessibility and provides information on how users can access your products and services. Both of these documents should be easily accessible and regularly updated to reflect your organization's ongoing efforts to improve accessibility.

- Develop accessibility guidelines for your team

Creating a set of internal accessibility guidelines will help your team members understand their roles and responsibilities when it comes to creating accessible digital products. These guidelines should be specific to your organization and the types of products and services you offer. They should also be aligned with established accessibility standards, such as the Web Content Accessibility Guidelines (WCAG).

- Maintain detailed records of accessibility testing and audits

Keeping thorough records of your accessibility testing and audits is crucial for tracking your progress and identifying areas for improvement. These records should include information on the testing methods used, the results of the tests, and any issues that were identified and resolved. Make sure to also document any updates and improvements made to your digital products as a result of the testing and audits.

- Create a centralized repository for accessibility resources

Having a centralized repository where your team can easily access and share accessibility resources, such as guidelines, checklists, and templates, can greatly improve the efficiency of your accessibility efforts. This repository can be a shared folder, an intranet site, or even a dedicated platform that allows team members to collaborate and contribute to the accessibility knowledge base.

- Regularly review and update your documentation

Accessibility is an ongoing process, and your documentation should reflect that. Regularly review and update your accessibility policy, guidelines, and other documentation to ensure they remain current and relevant. This will help your team stay informed about the latest accessibility best practices and will demonstrate your organization's commitment to continuous improvement.

- Share your progress and successes

Transparency is key when it comes to accessibility. Be open about your organization's progress in implementing accessibility initiatives and share your successes with your stakeholders, including customers, employees, and partners.

This can help to build trust and demonstrate your commitment to creating an inclusive digital environment.

- Seek feedback from users and stakeholders

Actively solicit feedback from your users and stakeholders on your digital products and your accessibility efforts. This feedback can provide valuable insights into areas for improvement and can help you to better understand the needs and preferences of your users.

conclusion

recap of key points and concepts

As we approach the end of our journey through the world of digital accessibility, it's essential to take a moment to review and consolidate the key points and concepts we've covered throughout this book. By doing so, we can ensure that these principles and practices become deeply ingrained in our approach to creating accessible digital products and services.

1.The importance of digital accessibility

At the heart of our discussion is the importance of digital accessibility. In today's increasingly connected world, it's crucial to ensure that everyone, including people with disabilities, can access and use digital products and services without barriers. By embracing accessibility, we promote inclusivity, adhere to legal requirements, and create a better overall experience for all users.

2. Understanding different types of disabilities

To design and develop accessible digital products, it's essential to understand the different types of disabilities that users may experience. We've covered various disabilities, including visual, auditory, cognitive, and motor impairments.

By considering the unique needs of users with these disabilities, we can create more inclusive digital experiences.

3.Universal design principles

Universal design principles emphasize the importance of creating products and services that are usable by as many people as possible, regardless of their abilities. By adhering to these principles, we can ensure that our digital products are not only accessible but also efficient and enjoyable for all users.

4. The Web Content Accessibility Guidelines (WCAG)

The WCAG is a set of guidelines that provide a comprehensive framework for making digital content accessible to users with disabilities. By following the WCAG, we can ensure that our digital products meet the highest standards of accessibility and comply with relevant laws and regulations.

5. Color theory and accessibility

An accessible color scheme is essential for users with visual impairments or color vision deficiencies. We've discussed the importance of choosing accessible color palettes, ensuring sufficient contrast, and using color to enhance, not hinder, the user experience.

6. Keyboard accessibility and focus management

Keyboard accessibility is vital for users who rely on keyboard navigation instead of a mouse. We've covered the importance of making all interactive elements accessible via the keyboard and managing focus to provide a seamless and efficient keyboard navigation experience.

7. Accessible menus and navigation patterns

Creating accessible menus and navigation patterns allows users to easily find and interact with the content they need. We've explored various techniques for designing accessible menus, including the use of ARIA roles and attributes, clear and concise labeling, and logical navigation structures.

8. Accessible forms and controls

Forms and controls are crucial components of many

digital products, and ensuring their accessibility is key. We've delved into best practices for designing accessible forms and controls, such as providing clear instructions, using appropriate input types, and ensuring proper error handling.

9. mage, video, and audio accessibility

Accessible media content is essential for users with visual or auditory impairments. We've discussed the importance of providing alternative text for images, captions and transcripts for videos, and audio descriptions to make multimedia content accessible to all users.

10. Accessible animations and interactive elements

Animations and interactive elements can enhance the user experience but may also create accessibility barriers if not properly designed. We've explored strategies for ensuring the accessibility of these elements, such as providing user control, minimizing motion and distractions, and ensuring keyboard accessibility.

11. Mobile and device accessibility

As mobile devices and various screen sizes become increasingly prevalent, it's crucial to ensure our digital products are accessible across different platforms. We've discussed touch and gesture accessibility, designing for different devices and screen sizes, and the importance of responsive design.

12. Testing and evaluation

Testing and evaluation are key components of creating accessible digital products. We've covered a range of testing techniques, including automated testing tools, manual testing, and inclusive user testing. We've also explored the value of accessibility audits and checklists for evaluating and improving accessibility throughout the development process.

13. Collaboration between designers, developers, and content creators

Creating accessible digital products requires collaboration between various team members, including designers, developers, and content creators. We've discussed the importance of establishing clear communication channels, sharing knowledge and resources, and working together to ensure that accessibility is integrated at every stage of the project.

14. Iterative design for continuous improvement

Accessibility is not a one-time effort but an ongoing process that requires continuous improvement. We've explored the concept of iterative design, which emphasizes the importance of regularly evaluating and refining digital products to ensure they remain accessible and responsive to the needs of all users.

15. Accessibility laws and regulations

Understanding and complying with accessibility laws and regulations is crucial for organizations to avoid legal and financial consequences. We've provided an overview of the key laws and regulations related to digital accessibility, including the Americans with Disabilities Act (ADA), the Web Content Accessibility Guidelines (WCAG), and the European Union's Web Accessibility Directive.

16. Meeting legal requirements

Meeting legal requirements for accessibility involves more than simply adhering to guidelines. We've discussed strategies for demonstrating compliance, such as conducting accessibility audits, creating accessibility statements, and providing accessible customer support.

17. Best practices for documentation and reporting

Clear and comprehensive documentation and reporting are essential components of an effective accessibility strategy. We've covered best practices for documenting and reporting accessibility efforts, including creating an accessibility statement, maintaining a record of testing and evaluation, and reporting progress to stakeholders.

encouragement to advocate for accessibility in ux design

Throughout this book, we've explored the numerous facets of digital accessibility and the importance of creating inclusive experiences for all users. As you've likely come to understand, accessibility is an essential aspect of UX design that cannot be overlooked. Yet, despite its importance, accessibility is still often seen as an afterthought or a box to be ticked in many organizations.

As a designer, developer, content creator, or anyone else involved in the creation of digital products and services, you have the power to change this narrative. By advocating for accessibility in your workplace and beyond, you can help shift perspectives, influence decision-makers, and create a more inclusive digital landscape. In this section, we'll discuss why advocacy is crucial and share some tips on how to become an effective accessibility advocate.

Why Advocate for Accessibility?

Accessibility advocacy is vital for several reasons:

1. Raising awareness: Many people are unaware of the challenges faced by individuals with disabilities when interacting with digital content. By advocating for accessibility, you can help educate others about these challenges and the importance of creating inclusive digital experiences.
2. Promoting empathy: When people understand the struggles faced by those with disabilities, they're more likely to empathize and prioritize accessibility in their design and development processes.
3. Driving change: Advocacy can lead to tangible improvements in the way organizations approach accessibility, resulting in more accessible products and services.

4. Fulfilling ethical obligations: As a professional involved in the creation of digital products and services, it's your ethical responsibility to ensure that your work is accessible to all users.

Now that we understand the importance of advocacy let's explore some tips for becoming an effective accessibility advocate.

Tips for Effective Accessibility Advocacy

1. Educate yourself: Before you can effectively advocate for accessibility, it's essential to have a solid understanding of the principles, guidelines, and best practices. Keep learning and expanding your knowledge on accessibility, as it's an ever-evolving field.
2. Share your knowledge: Share your accessibility knowledge with colleagues, clients, and decision-makers. Offer to give presentations or workshops, write blog posts or articles, and participate in relevant online discussions.
3. Be patient and persistent: Changing organizational attitudes and processes takes time. Be patient with those who may not initially understand the importance of accessibility, and be persistent in your efforts to drive change.
4. Lead by example: Demonstrate your commitment to accessibility by incorporating it into your work and processes. When others see your dedication, they're more likely to follow suit.
5. Collaborate with others: Accessibility is a team effort. Collaborate with colleagues across disciplines, share your insights, and learn from one another.

6. Network with accessibility professionals: Connect with others who share your passion for accessibility. Join online forums, attend conferences and webinars, and participate in local meetups. These connections can help you stay informed and provide valuable support in your advocacy efforts.
7. Communicate the benefits: When advocating for accessibility, it's important to emphasize the benefits for everyone, not just individuals with disabilities. Highlight the improved user experience, increased audience reach, and potential legal and financial benefits of creating accessible digital products and services.
8. Celebrate successes: When your advocacy efforts lead to improvements in accessibility, celebrate those achievements. Recognizing progress can help build momentum and inspire others to prioritize accessibility.

In the quest to create a more inclusive digital landscape, your role as an accessibility advocate is invaluable. By championing accessibility in your workplace and beyond, you can help ensure that everyone, regardless of their abilities, has the opportunity to access and engage with digital content.

As you continue on your accessibility journey, consider the following actions to maintain your momentum and expand your impact:

1. Stay informed: Keep up with the latest developments, news, and research related to accessibility. Subscribe to newsletters, follow industry leaders on social media, and join relevant online communities.
2. Seek feedback: Regularly ask for feedback on your accessibility efforts from colleagues, clients, and

users with disabilities. This feedback will help you identify areas for improvement and provide opportunities for growth.

3. Measure progress: Establish benchmarks and track your progress in implementing accessibility best practices. Regularly evaluate your projects to ensure you're meeting your accessibility goals and making continuous improvements.
4. Advocate outside your organization: Share your accessibility expertise and experiences with other professionals, both within and outside your industry. By doing so, you can help spread awareness and inspire others to prioritize accessibility.
5. Engage with the disability community: Connect with individuals with disabilities and organizations that represent them. Listen to their experiences and insights, and involve them in your accessibility efforts whenever possible.
6. Be adaptable: The field of digital accessibility is always evolving. Be open to change and adapt your approach as new technologies, standards, and best practices emerge.

Remember, you're not alone in your pursuit of creating a more accessible digital world. There are countless others who share your passion and dedication. By working together, we can create a more inclusive digital landscape that ensures no one is left behind.

In this book, we've covered a wide range of topics related to accessibility, from color palettes and keyboard accessibility to inclusive user testing and legal requirements. As you apply these principles and best practices to your work, remember that accessibility is about more than just meeting guidelines and avoiding legal issues. It's about creating a digital world that is welcoming, usable, and enjoyable for everyone.

ongoing learning and resources

Embarking on a journey to master accessibility in UX design is both exciting and rewarding. As we've explored throughout this book, the field of accessibility is vast and continually evolving. To be an effective advocate and practitioner, it's essential to commit to ongoing learning and staying informed about the latest developments and best practices. In this section, we'll highlight some valuable resources and strategies to help you stay up-to-date and continue refining your skills.

1. Online courses and certifications

Investing time in professional development can help deepen your understanding of accessibility concepts and practices. There are numerous online courses available, ranging from free introductory lessons to in-depth, paid programs that offer certification upon completion. Some well-regarded options include:

- W3C Web Accessibility Initiative (WAI) resources: WAI offers a wealth of free online tutorials, guidelines, and checklists on various accessibility topics.
- WebAIM: WebAIM provides comprehensive training on web accessibility, including workshops, webinars, and online courses.
- Deque University: Deque offers a range of online courses and certifications in web accessibility, as well as resources like articles and webinars.
- Google Accessibility Fundamentals: This free course from Google covers key accessibility

principles and techniques for web and Android development.

- Blogs, podcasts, and YouTube channels

Following blogs, podcasts, and YouTube channels dedicated to accessibility can help you stay informed about new trends, tools, and techniques. Some notable resources include:

- A11y Project: This community-driven effort offers a collection of articles, resources, and tools related to web accessibility.
- Inclusive Components: This blog explores various UI patterns and offers practical advice on making them accessible.
- Accessibility Weekly: This newsletter curates the latest news and articles in the accessibility field.
- A11y Rules Podcast: This podcast features interviews with accessibility experts, sharing their insights and experiences.

- Conferences and workshops

Attending conferences and workshops can be an excellent way to learn from industry experts, network with other professionals, and stay updated on accessibility advancements. Some popular accessibility-focused events include:

- CSUN Assistive Technology Conference: This annual event is one of the largest conferences dedicated to assistive technology and accessibility.
- AccessU: This conference and training event offers hands-on workshops, presentations, and networking opportunities for accessibility professionals.

- WebAIM Training: WebAIM conducts regular workshops and training events, both online and in-person.

- Social media and online communities

Engaging with accessibility-focused social media accounts and online communities can provide valuable insights, discussions, and support. Consider following accessibility experts on platforms like Twitter and LinkedIn, and joining forums and groups dedicated to accessibility, such as:

- WebAIM Mailing List: This active mailing list allows subscribers to ask questions and discuss accessibility topics with other professionals.
- /r/accessibility: This Reddit community is a space for sharing resources, asking questions, and discussing accessibility-related topics.
- Web Accessibility Slack: This Slack group is dedicated to web accessibility, providing a platform for networking and knowledge sharing.

- Books and academic research

Finally, don't overlook the value of books and academic research in deepening your understanding of accessibility. Some essential reads on this topic include:

- "Don't Make Me Think" by Steve Krug: This classic UX design book includes a section on accessibility best practices.
- "A Web for Everyone" by Sarah Horton and Whitney Quesenbery: This comprehensive guide covers a range of accessibility topics and offers practical advice for designers and developers.

- "Universal Design for Web Applications" by Wendy Chisholm and Matt May: This book focuses on universal design principles and their application to web development.

As you continue your journey in the world of accessibility, remember that learning is an ongoing process. Stay curious, be open to new ideas, and never underestimate the impact your work can have on creating a more inclusive digital landscape. By staying connected to the accessibility community, sharing your knowledge with others, and engaging in professional development, you'll not only improve your own skills but also help shape a more accessible future for everyone.

In addition to these resources, it's crucial to actively seek feedback from users and collaborate with colleagues to ensure your designs are truly accessible. Solicit input from people with diverse abilities, and listen to their experiences and suggestions. By doing so, you'll gain invaluable insights into how your designs can better meet the needs of a wide range of users.

Another important aspect of ongoing learning is to stay informed about changes in accessibility laws and regulations. As digital accessibility becomes an increasingly important societal concern, it's likely that legal requirements will continue to evolve. Staying abreast of these changes will help you ensure your designs remain compliant and avoid potential legal complications.

Finally, don't forget the importance of celebrating your successes and learning from your mistakes. As you implement accessible design practices and see the positive impact on your users, take the time to acknowledge your progress and share your experiences with others. By doing so, you'll not only reinforce your own commitment to accessibility but also inspire and motivate others to join the cause.

The journey to becoming an accessibility advocate and

expert is a rewarding one, filled with opportunities for growth and the satisfaction of knowing your work is making a tangible difference in people's lives. By staying informed, embracing a growth mindset, and fostering a spirit of collaboration, you can help create a more inclusive and accessible world for all.

Remember that accessibility is not just a one-time effort, but an ongoing commitment to ensuring that everyone can fully experience and engage with digital content. By staying dedicated to this cause and continuing to learn and grow, you'll be well-equipped to face the challenges and opportunities that lie ahead in the ever-evolving world of UX design.

We hope that this book has provided you with valuable insights and tools to help you on your accessibility journey. As you continue to learn and grow, we encourage you to share your knowledge, experiences, and passion for accessibility with others. Together, we can create a more inclusive digital landscape for everyone to enjoy.

appendices

glossary of accessibility terms

Welcome to the glossary of accessibility terms! This section will introduce you to the key terminology used throughout the book, providing you with a handy reference for understanding and discussing accessibility topics. While some of these terms may already be familiar to you, others might be new or less commonly used. We hope this glossary will serve as a useful tool as you deepen your knowledge of accessibility in UX design.

1. A11y: A numeronym for "accessibility." The 11 represents the number of letters between the first 'a' and the last 'y' in the word "accessibility."
2. Accessible Rich Internet Applications (ARIA): A set of attributes that define ways to make web content and web applications more accessible to people with disabilities. ARIA helps with dynamic content and advanced user interface controls developed with Ajax, HTML, JavaScript, and related technologies.

3. Alt Text: Short for "alternative text," alt text is a description of an image that is displayed when the image cannot be rendered or is not available, and is read by screen readers to provide context to users who are visually impaired.
4. Assistive Technology: Devices, software, or equipment that help people with disabilities access, navigate, and interact with digital content. Examples include screen readers, screen magnifiers, and speech recognition software.
5. Audio Description: A narration track that provides a description of the visual elements of a video or multimedia presentation, making it accessible to people who are blind or have low vision.
6. Captions: Text versions of the audio content in a video or multimedia presentation, synchronized with the visual content, which enable people who are deaf or hard of hearing to understand the audio portion of the content.
7. Color Contrast: The difference in brightness and color between the foreground (such as text) and background elements in a design. Adequate color contrast is essential for ensuring that users with low vision or color vision deficiencies can easily read and understand content.
8. Focus Management: The practice of ensuring that users can navigate and interact with web content using only a keyboard or other input device, by controlling the order and visibility of interactive elements that receive focus.
9. Inclusive Design: A design approach that considers the full range of human diversity, including but not limited to disability, and seeks to create products and experiences that can be used and enjoyed by as many people as possible.

10. Keyboard Accessibility: The ability for users to navigate and interact with web content using only a keyboard, without the need for a mouse or other pointing device. This is important for users with motor impairments or those who rely on assistive technologies like screen readers.
11. Long Description: A detailed text description of a complex image or graphic that cannot be adequately described using alt text alone. Long descriptions are typically provided as a separate link or hidden text that can be accessed by screen readers.
12. Mobile Accessibility: The practice of ensuring that websites, apps, and other digital content are accessible and user-friendly on mobile devices, taking into account factors such as touch input, small screen sizes, and varying device capabilities.
13. Screen Reader: A software application that converts text and other on-screen content into synthesized speech, allowing people who are blind or visually impaired to access and interact with digital content.
14. Semantic Markup: The use of HTML elements to provide meaning and context to web content, making it more understandable and navigable for users and assistive technologies.
15. Skip Links: Navigation links placed at the beginning of a web page that allow users to bypass repetitive content (such as headers and navigation menus) and quickly access the main content of the page.
16. Transcripts: Text versions of the spoken content in an audio or video file, which provide access to the information for users who are deaf or hard of hearing, as well Universal Design: A design approach that seeks to create products,

environments, and experiences that can be used and enjoyed by everyone, regardless of age, ability, or circumstance. Universal design often overlaps with inclusive design and accessibility.

17. Usability: The extent to which a product, system, or interface can be used effectively and efficiently by a wide range of users to achieve their goals.
18. User Experience (UX): The overall experience a person has when interacting with a product or system, encompassing all aspects of the interaction, including usability, accessibility, and emotional factors.
19. VoiceOver: A screen reader built into Apple's iOS, macOS, and other operating systems, which provides spoken feedback and allows users who are blind or visually impaired to interact with their devices.
20. WCAG (Web Content Accessibility Guidelines): A set of guidelines and best practices for creating accessible web content, developed by the World Wide Web Consortium (W3C). WCAG is organized into three levels of conformance (A, AA, and AAA), with Level A being the minimum and Level AAA being the most comprehensive.
21. WebAIM (Web Accessibility in Mind): A nonprofit organization that provides resources, training, and guidance on web accessibility, including the popular "WebAIM Checklist" for evaluating and improving the accessibility of web content.
22. ZoomText: A screen magnification and screen reading software for users with low vision, which allows them to enlarge and enhance on-screen content for easier viewing and navigation.

accessibility checklists and guidelines

Welcome to the section on accessibility checklists and guidelines! Here, we will explore some of the most commonly used and trusted resources for ensuring your designs are accessible and inclusive. Following established guidelines and using checklists can help you systematically evaluate your work and identify areas for improvement. Let's dive in and learn about these valuable resources.

1.Web Content Accessibility Guidelines (WCAG)

The Web Content Accessibility Guidelines, or WCAG, is a set of recommendations developed by the World Wide Web Consortium (W3C) to make web content more accessible. These guidelines are organized into three levels of conformance: Level A, Level AA, and Level AAA. Level A represents the minimum level of accessibility, while Level AAA is the highest standard.

Each level has a series of criteria, known as success criteria, which are organized under four principles: Perceivable, Operable, Understandable, and Robust (POUR). By addressing the success criteria in your designs, you can make your content more accessible to a wider audience, including people with disabilities.

- W3C's Accessible Rich Internet Applications (ARIA)

ARIA is a technical specification developed by W3C to improve the accessibility of web content and applications, particularly for users with disabilities. ARIA provides a set of attributes that can be added to HTML elements to enhance their semantics and make them more accessible to assistive technologies like screen readers. ARIA can be especially useful for creating accessible widgets, navigation menus, and other interactive elements.

- WebAIM's WCAG 2 Checklist

WebAIM, a nonprofit organization focused on web accessibility, has created a handy WCAG 2 Checklist to help you evaluate and improve the accessibility of your web content. The checklist is organized by the four POUR principles and covers Level A and Level AA conformance. This resource can be a great starting point for assessing your website's accessibility and identifying areas that need improvement.

- Section 508 Standards

In the United States, the Section 508 Standards are part of the Rehabilitation Act, which requires federal agencies to make their electronic and information technology accessible to people with disabilities. The Section 508 Standards cover a wide range of technologies, including websites, software applications, and electronic documents. Although these standards are specific to federal agencies, they can also serve as a helpful resource for designers and developers working on any project.

- Mobile Accessibility Guidelines

As mobile devices become increasingly important in our daily lives, it's essential to ensure that mobile apps and websites are accessible as well. The Mobile Web Best Practices and the Mobile Accessibility Guidelines, both developed by the W3C, offer guidance on creating accessible mobile content. These guidelines address issues like touch target size, device orientation, and gesture support.

- Inclusive Design Toolkit

The Inclusive Design Toolkit, developed by Microsoft,

provides a set of principles and practices for creating accessible and inclusive products. This toolkit includes guidelines for color contrast, typography, layout, and interaction design, as well as resources for conducting inclusive user research and testing.

- Cognitive Accessibility Guidelines

For users with cognitive disabilities, it's essential to create content that is easy to understand and navigate. The Cognitive Accessibility Guidelines, developed by the W3C, offer strategies for simplifying content, enhancing navigation, and providing support for users who may struggle with memory, focus, or problem-solving.

additional resources and tools for accessible ux design

As we've journeyed through the world of accessible UX design, we've touched on numerous techniques, tools, and resources to help make your designs more inclusive. In this section, we'll delve into additional resources and tools that can further support you in creating accessible user experiences. These resources can serve as useful companions on your quest to build a more inclusive digital world.

WebAIM (Web Accessibility in Mind)

- WebAIM is an invaluable resource for web designers and developers looking to enhance the accessibility of their work. The organization offers a wealth of information, from articles and tutorials to guidelines and checklists. Their WCAG 2 checklist is particularly helpful for ensuring your designs meet accessibility standards. Visit their website at https://webaim.org/.

The A11Y Project

- The A11Y Project is a community-driven effort to make web accessibility easier. Their website includes resources such as checklists, patterns, and tips for creating accessible content. The site also features a blog with insights and advice from accessibility experts. Check out their website at https://www.a11yproject.com/.

WAI-ARIA Authoring Practices

- WAI-ARIA (Web Accessibility Initiative - Accessible Rich Internet Applications) Authoring Practices is a guide for understanding how to create accessible web content with ARIA. It offers examples, explanations, and best practices for using ARIA roles, states, and properties in your designs. Visit the WAI-ARIA Authoring Practices website at https://www.w3.org/TR/wai-aria-practices/.

Color Contrast Analyzers

- To ensure your designs have sufficient color contrast, there are several tools available, such as the WebAIM Color Contrast Checker (https://webaim.org/resources/contrastchecker/) and the Colorable tool (https://colorable.jxnblk.com/). These tools allow you to quickly evaluate and adjust the color contrast of your designs to meet accessibility standards.

Accessibility Linters and Browser Extensions

- Using accessibility linters and browser extensions can help you identify accessibility issues during the development process. Some popular options include aXe by Deque Systems (https://www.deque.com/axe/) and the Accessibility Insights extension for Chrome and Edge (https://accessibilityinsights.io/). These tools can help you catch potential problems early on, making it easier to address them before your designs go live.

Inclusive Components

- Inclusive Components is a blog by Heydon Pickering that explores different UI components and offers insights into how they can be made more accessible. Each post includes code examples and explanations of the accessibility considerations for that specific component. You can find the blog at https://inclusive-components.design/.

WAVE (Web Accessibility Evaluation Tool)

1. WAVE is an online tool developed by WebAIM that evaluates the accessibility of your web pages. Simply enter the URL of the page you'd like to evaluate, and WAVE will provide you with a detailed report of any accessibility issues it finds, along with suggestions for improvement. Give it a try at https://wave.webaim.org/.

Smashing Magazine's Accessibility Category

- Smashing Magazine is a popular web design and development publication that regularly features articles on accessibility. Their accessibility category is a treasure trove of information, featuring a variety of articles written by experts in the field. Browse the category at https://www.smashingmagazine.com/category/accessibility/.

Accessibility Conferences and Workshops

- Attending accessibility conferences and workshops can help you deepen your understanding of accessible UX design and connect with others in the field. Some notable events include the International Association of Accessibility Professionals (IAAP) Global Accessibility Conference, the CSUN Assistive Technology Conference, and the A11y Camp.

As you continue to explore and implement accessible UX design practices, these resources and tools can serve as valuable allies in your journey. Remember, creating accessible designs is an ongoing process, and staying informed and up-to-date is essential to ensuring your work remains inclusive.

Accessible Design Courses and Certifications

- Investing in your education is one of the best ways to deepen your understanding of accessible UX design. Many organizations offer courses and certifications, such as the International Association of Accessibility Professionals (IAAP), which provides the Certified Professional in Accessibility Core Competencies (CPACC) and Web Accessibility Specialist (WAS) certifications. Additionally, online learning platforms like Coursera, Udemy, and LinkedIn Learning offer a range of accessibility courses taught by industry professionals.

Online Communities and Forums

- Participating in online communities and forums dedicated to accessibility can provide you with a wealth of knowledge, support, and inspiration. Some popular options include the WebAIM mailing list, the A11y Slack group, and the Accessibility subreddit (https://www.reddit.com/r/accessibility/). These communities are a great place to ask questions, share resources, and learn from others who share your passion for accessible design.

Accessibility Guidelines and Standards

- Familiarizing yourself with accessibility guidelines and standards is crucial in creating accessible designs. Some key guidelines include the Web Content Accessibility Guidelines (WCAG), the Authoring Tool Accessibility Guidelines (ATAG), and the User Agent Accessibility Guidelines (UAAG). These guidelines provide a framework for understanding and implementing accessibility best practices.

Books on Accessibility

- There are many books available that focus on accessibility, covering topics such as inclusive design, web accessibility, and mobile accessibility. Some notable titles include "Inclusive Design Patterns" by Heydon Pickering, "A Web for Everyone" by Sarah Horton and Whitney Quesenbery, and "Apps for All: Coding Accessible Web Applications" by Heydon Pickering. These books can provide you with a solid foundation for understanding and implementing accessible UX design principles.

Accessibility Blogs and Podcasts

- To stay current on accessibility trends and best practices, consider following accessibility-focused blogs and podcasts. Some popular options include the A11y Rules Podcast, the Simply Accessible blog, and the blog at Deque Systems. These resources can provide you with regular updates and insights into the world of accessible UX design.

As we wrap up this section, it's worth remembering that accessibility is not a destination but a journey. Embrace the process of continuous learning and improvement, and always strive to create the most inclusive designs possible. Use the resources and tools mentioned in this section as a starting point, and keep exploring and discovering new ways to make your work more accessible. By doing so, you'll be making a significant impact on the lives of countless individuals and contributing to a more inclusive digital world. Stay curious, stay informed, and continue to be an advocate for accessible UX design. Together, we can make a difference.

www.ingramcontent.com/pod-product-compliance
Lightning Source LLC
LaVergne TN
LVHW090357210926
848480LV00002B/375